The Monomyth Reboot

The Monomyth Reboot

A Transmodern Update for Mythopoeia

Nadia Salem

LEXINGTON BOOKS
Lanham • Boulder • New York • London

Rowman & Littlefield
Bloomsbury Publishing Inc, 1359 Broadway, New York, NY 10018, USA
Bloomsbury Publishing Plc, 50 Bedford Square, London, WC1B 3DP, UK
Bloomsbury Publishing Ireland, 29 Earlsfort Terrace, Dublin 2, D02 AY28, Ireland
www.bloomsbury.com

Published by Lexington Books
An imprint of The Rowman & Littlefield Publishing Group, Inc.
4501 Forbes Boulevard, Suite 200, Lanham, Maryland 20706
www.rowman.com
86-90 Paul Street, London EC2A 4NE, United Kingdom

British Library Cataloguing in Publication Information available

Library of Congress Cataloging-in-Publication Data
Names: Salem, Nadia, 1973- author.
Title: The monomyth reboot : a transmodern update for mythopoeia / Nadia Salem.
Description: Lanham : Lexington Books, 2024. | Includes bibliographical references
    and index. | Summary: "In this book, Nadia Salem expands the standardized mythic
    quest of the hero's journey for storytellers to include the heroine's journey. By arguing
    that the former reflects coming of age while the latter coming of middle-age, Salem
    reveals how both are integral to depictions of fully developed characters"—Provided
    by publisher.
Identifiers: LCCN 2023038268 (print) | LCCN 2023038269 (ebook) | ISBN
    9781793648075 (cloth) | ISBN 9781793648099 (pbk) | ISBN 9781793648082 (epub)
Subjects: LCSH: Myth in literature. | Women heroes in literature. | Characters and
    characteristics in literature.
Classification: LCC PN56.M94 S25 2024 (print) | LCC PN56.M94 (ebook) |
    DDC 809/.915—dc23/eng/20230919
LC record available at https://lccn.loc.gov/2023038268
LC ebook record available at https://lccn.loc.gov/2023038269

Contents

Preface

This book is about the monomyth, the mid-twentieth- century idea put forth by Joseph Campbell that all heroic myths could be boiled down to a limited number of common steps, evidencing a universal journey repeated across time and cultures. His theory, however, was beset with broad, unproven claims and criticisms, eventually amounting to nothing more than a curiosity to be explored by intrepid storytellers. By the twenty-first century, his theory was academically dismissed and relegated to the dustbins of yesteryear as a relic of modernism in a postmodern world. And yet, George Lucas took exception to this view. Standing up against scholarly critique on one end and the budgetary demands of Hollywood studios on the other (to the far extent of accepting a pay cut if he failed), George Lucas wrote from the sci-fi margins of the film world with complete commitment to the monomyth. In talking about the making of *Star Wars* (1977), he says:

> I realized before I did *Star Wars* that there was no contemporary fairy tale and that the number of parents who sit down and tell their children fairy tales is dwindling. As families begin to break up, kids are left more to the television and they don't hear bedtime stories. As a result, people are learning their mythology from TV, which makes them very confused because it has no point of view, no sense of morality. Fairy tales, religion, all were designed to teach the right way to live and give a moral anchor.[1]

Plagued with production problems, George Lucas's expectation for success dwindled with rising costs. "I was working on the assumption as every film-maker works on, which is the film would be a disaster and that it won't be promoted and it'll just die a horrible death."[2] But the film opens to unprecedented success and soon surpasses *Jaws* (1975) as the number one film of all time, while filmgoers stood in long lines at early hours to see it all over the world. It's nominated for eleven Academy Awards and wins seven. As an early fan, Stephen Colbert says of the time, "*Star Wars* came out and we went to school the next day unable to explain to our friends how everything was different now."[3] When adjusted for inflation, *Star Wars*, later renamed *Star Wars: Episode IV—A New Hope*, remains the second highest grossing film of all time (after *Gone with the Wind* (1939)), generating numerous prequels, sequels, spinoffs, and anthologies, and leaving an indelible mark on fandom, filmmakers, and storytellers.[4] During retirement in 2012, Lucas sold Lucasfilm, the company he founded to make *Star Wars*, to The Walt Disney Company for over $4 billion dollars and dedicated the proceeds to an educational charity.[5] According to film producer Howard Kazanjian, "[George Lucas] really established the independent film market. His films changed epic productions. He changed storytelling. He created what Hollywood is today."[6]

Contemporary filmmakers attribute their inspiration to *Star Wars*. Peter Jackson, producer and director of the Academy Award- winning *Lord of the Rings* trilogy (2001–2003), says:

> I remember standing and cheering and waving my arms around when Luke was flying toward the Death Star. I remember being incredibly overwrought at the excitement of it all. That sort of stuff didn't happen in films back then. It was probably the first time in my life I'd ever become that heavily engaged in a movie to the point of wanting to jump up and down and yell for the hero. It connected. It was a movie that was incredibly successful at engaging us. Luke really was us. That was Luke's great contribution to the story of *Star Wars*. He was the character who you felt you could relate to—he wasn't outside of your reach. Luke was just a kid like us who was swept away in this adventure—and though incredible things were asked of him, he managed to find it within himself to deliver in the way that we all hoped, if we were flying that X-wing toward the Death Star. Certainly at the time, I don't think I'd ever seen a movie that was as successful at picking you up out of your seat and plunking you right down in the film. Another real feature of its success was that *Star Wars* spoke to you in a truthful way.[7]

Steven Spielberg, producer and director of *Jaws*, *E.T. the Extra-Terrestrial* (1982), and the *Indiana Jones* series (1981–2023), recalls that "George tapped into something very spiritual for young and old. *Star Wars* is a deeply spiritual story, yet somehow he made a war movie, too, and created a mythology of characters—he touched something that needed touching in everybody."[8] James Cameron, director of *Titanic* (1997), *Avatar* (2009), and *Terminator* (1984), (*Titanic* holds the fifth spot for highest grossing film adjusted for inflation),[9] quit his job as a truck driver after watching *Star Wars* and pursued filmmaking.[10] According to the director of *Boyz n the Hood* (1991) and *Four Brothers* (2005), John Singleton, "Anyone who knows me knows that my life was changed at that moment" at the age of nine.[11] By 2017, fans had spent over $262 billion dollars on *Star Wars* franchise merchandise.[12] Some fans have even taken "Jediism" as a form of faith. Professor of Religious Studies, John Lyden, observes that, "If there is any popular culture phenomenon that can be referred to as 'religion,' it would be the fandom associated with the *Star Wars* films. In the 2001 census in many English-speaking countries, a number of people identified their religion as 'Jediism,' including 70,000 in Australia, 21,000 in Canada, 53,000 in New Zealand, and 390,127 in England and Wales."[13]

What is it about *Star Wars* that inspired so many? After interviewing Joseph Campbell, Bill Moyers recalls that "Joseph Campbell said to me the best student he ever had was George Lucas."[14] Following in the footsteps of the monomyth, Lucas became a myth-maker. Writing in the summer of the movie's release in the *Journal of Popular Culture*, Robert Collins notes:

> [A]nother and more significant reason for [*Star Wars's*] success is its particular nature as a narrative epic. [. . .] [It] demonstrates a need, and a growing desire, for positive myth, a force to bolster the life patterns of common man. "Humankind," in T.S. Eliot's famous phrase, "cannot bear too much reality," and since World War II even popular fare has been a heavy dose of cynicism, pessimism, and the ugly truth. The pendulum nears another swing: we are ready—more than ready, eager—for mythic heroes. *Star Wars*, on any other grounds is inexplicable; taken for what it is, it functions as magic. With incredible audacity, it combines the stereotypes of modern pop literature and cinema with Arthurian romance. Lucas deliberately and obviously steals from such movie antecedents as the original *Wizard of Oz*, from the classic movie and pulp westerns based on the frontier tradition, from the old World War I and World War II flying battles. In fact, it is done so deliberately that a second considerations (sic) forces one to drop the word "steal" and substitute another verb; Lucas weaves together these elements of modern myth and ties to earlier ones that have long since embedded themselves in our historical consciousness. The result is a new and effective narrative technique.[15]

However, this technique is not new. It's known as *mythopoesis*, deriving from the Greek words *mythos,* meaning "myth," and *poieo*, meaning "to make." Myths have been used to explain the world around us, teach moral lessons, inspire the distressed, touch the human spirit, and entertain audiences. Mythopoesis farms mythology to explore the human experience, provide insight into the human psyche, and make sense of the world based on an assumption that myths transcend culture and time when speaking about the human condition. And it's not restricted to ancient mythology. Drawing inspiration from modern myth-makers like J.R.R. Tolkien, C.S. Lewis, J.K. Rowling, or George Lucas to create new myths is also a form of myth-making. Mythopoesis has been practiced for centuries, dating back to the earliest narrative in recorded history from the third millennium BCE in ancient Mesopotamia—the Epic of Gilgamesh, narrating the tale of a king in pursuit of immortality which has been subsequently retold and adapted countless times, with Gilgamesh serving as a precursor to Hercules.[16]

In ancient Greece, Homer harnesses a rich mythological tradition to create a complex narrative in the *Iliad* and the *Odyssey* by using motifs of heroes and archetypes with themes of bravery and honor to depict struggle against overwhelming odds and victory over impossible challenges. The *Iliad* utilizes the legend of the Trojan horse which in the course of time metamorphizes into a motif. In ancient China, the Taoist pantheon includes many gods and goddesses, such as the Jade Emperor and the Queen Mother of the West, who are the subject of numerous myths and legends, while in ancient India, parables of Hindu gods and goddesses have been passed down through generations in oral and written form. The *Mahabharata* uses gods, heroes, and monsters to impart spiritual and philosophical wisdom by telling an epic story of a great war between two families. The *Mahabharata* along with another BCE epic poem, the *Ramayana*, have been retold and adapted in many different modes over the centuries, from literature to film and television.

In the Middle Ages, Dante Alighieri's *Divine Comedy* and John Milton's *Paradise Lost* tap into Christian mythology to teach moral lessons and explore human purpose that would endure for centuries. In Japan, the eleventh century classic *The Tale of Genji* tells the story of the life and loves of a prince by incorporating Japanese mythology and culture and has been adapted and reinterpreted numerous times. The art of mythopoesis is practiced in the *One Thousand and One Nights*, a collection of tales from the Islamic world, which retells legends of Aladdin, Ali Baba, and Sinbad the Sailor, and continues to be repurposed in each successive generation.

In the modern era, mythopoesis has continued to evolve in changing cultural contexts. The works of J.R.R. Tolkien present a prime example of modern mythopoesis. He believes in mythopoesis famously arguing with C.S. Lewis that myths are not lies any more than names are.[17] Inspired by this argument, he later pens the poem "Mythopoeia," from Philomythos (the myth-lover) to Misomythus (the myth-hater).[18] "You look at trees and label them just so."[19] But "trees are not 'trees,'" until they are seen and named, and the naming process may be as phantasmic as myth-making or as real.[20] Both are splintered from divine truth and created by human, fallible language. Post-Jungian psychologist James Hillman asserts that even therapy utilizes mythopoesis. "[T]herapy pretends to being creative, and I use that word advisedly to mean originating of significative imaginative patterns, poeisis. Successful therapy is thus a collaboration between fictions, a revisioning of the story into a more intelligent, more imaginative plot, which also means the sense of mythos in all the parts of the story."[21]

Mythopoesis involves the process of drawing on motifs, structures, styles, rhythms, archetypes of ancient or modern myths, legends, or fairy tales to create a world that speaks to profound aspects of the human condition and conveys deeper themes such as the struggle for identity, the clash between the past and present, the profane versus the sacred, good versus evil, the search for meaning and purpose, mortality and immortality, and the quest to transform and transcend one's self or universe. For the purposes of this study, I focus on the mythopoeic works of Eros and Psyche, *Jane Eyre*, and *Titanic*. Eros and Psyche is an epic love story deriving from Greek mythology, first appearing in Apuleius's *Metamorphoses* in the second century CE. Eros is the renowned Greek and Roman (as Cupid) god of love, appearing in myths as early as Hesiod's *Theogony* in 700 BCE. Scholars have argued that Eros and Psyche retells local lore from an oral history.[22] Charlotte Brontë's *Jane Eyre*, which has been in continuous print since its publication in 1847, retells the Greek myth of Eros and Psyche and itself is retold over 100 times in the twentieth century, in the mediums of silent films, sound films, radio, television, theatre, and novels as prequels, sequels, and remakes. Perhaps the greatest retelling of Eros and Psyche can be found 150 years later, in James Cameron's *Titanic*, which quickly became the highest grossing film of all time, after its release in 1997 and remains the fourth highest grossing film worldwide (unadjusted for inflation), beaten out by Cameron's other two films, *Avatar* at #1 and *Avatar: The Way of Water* at #3 in 2023.[23] Neither Charlotte Brontë nor James Cameron have confessed to borrowing from the Greek myth, but an analysis through the lens of the monomyth reveals a similar pattern in all three that has transcended time, culture, and medium.

This begs the question then, how? George Lucas, who was inspired by the monomyth, highlights that "I did research to try to distill everything down into motifs that would be universal. I attribute most of the success to the psychological underpinnings which had been around for thousands of years and the people still react the same way to the stories as they always had."[24] The monomyth explains the pattern of the hero's journey, but the reason it's true, according to Campbell, is based in psychology. Oscillating between Freud and Jung for justification, Campbell actually never fully clarifies how or why Freudian or Jungian psychology supports the monomyth. For the purposes of this book, I take up this question and focus on how Jungian and post-Jungian psychology illuminates a psychological imperative behind a hero undertaking such a journey. To be clear, this is not a book on Jung and film, Jung and literature, or Jung and mythology although it adds to those canons. The investigations undertaken into analytical psychology's conceptions of individuation serve to fill a lacuna left by Campbell in reference to the psychological footings of the monomyth. I explore the problems of the monomyth as articulated by critics and then propose a re-envisioning of its steps more closely aligned with individuation as a possible solution. I then use a myth, a novel, and a movie as case studies to probe the practice of the monomyth as rebooted across the genres and in different periods.

This book is intended for creatives, the educators of creatives, researchers in media and film studies, mythology, and depth psychology, as well as any student of story.

NOTES

1. J. W. Rinzler, *The Making of Star Wars, The Empire Strikes Back: The Definitive Story* (New York: Del Rey Books, 2010), 12.

2. Kevin Burns, *Empire of Dreams: The Story of the Star Wars Trilogy* (20th Century Fox Television, 2004), featuring George Lucas, Carrie Fisher, Harrison Ford, Mark Hamill, Bill Moyers, Steven Spielberg, Walter Cronkite, Robert Clotworthy, Anthony Daniels, Warwick Davis, https://www.disneyplus.com/movies/empire-of -dreams-the-story-of-the-star-wars-trilogy/zTcS6xwUFnKx.

3. Kevin Burns, *Star Wars: The Legacy Revealed* (Prometheus Entertainment, The History Channel, and Lucasfilm Ltd, 2007), Documentary.

4. "Top Lifetime Adjusted Grosses," Box Office Mojo by IMDB Pro, updated March 2, 2023, accessed March 2, 2023, https://www.boxofficemojo.com/chart/top _lifetime_gross_adjusted/?adjust_gross_to=2022.

5. Alex Ben Block, "George Lucas Will Use Disney $4 Billion to Fund Education," *The Hollywood Reporter*, October 12, 2012, https://www.hollywoodreporter.com/ news/general-news/disney-deal-george-lucas-will-384947/.

6. Burns, *Empire of Dreams: The Story of the Star Wars Trilogy*.

7. J. W. Rinzler, *The Making of Star Wars (Enhanced Edition)* (New York: Random House Worlds, 2013), 16-18.

8. Rinzler, *The Making of Star Wars (Enhanced Edition)*, 1438.

9. "Top Lifetime Adjusted Grosses."

10. Rinzler, *The Making of Star Wars (Enhanced Edition)*, 1436.

11. Rinzler, *The Making of Star Wars (Enhanced Edition)*, 1439.

12. Dave McNary, "'Star Wars' Movies Push Overall Licensed Merchandise Sales to $262 Billion," *Variety* (May 22, 2017). https://variety.com/2017/film/news/star -wars-movies-licensed-merchandise-1202438161/.

13. John C. Lyden, "Whose Film Is It, Anyway? Canonicity and Authority in 'Star Wars' Fandom," *Journal of the American Academy of Religion* 80, no. 3 (2012): 775, https://doi.org/10.1093/jaarel/lfs037.

14. Burns, *Empire of Dreams: The Story of the Star Wars Trilogy*.

15. Robert G. Collins, "*Star Wars*: The Pastiche of Myth and the Yearning For A Past Future," *Journal of Popular Culture* 11, no. 1 (Summer 1977).

16. Robert K. G. Temple, *He Who Saw Everything: A Verse Translation of the Epic of Gilgamesh* (London: Rider, 1991), viii. According to Temple, "The tradition of heroic sagas takes its ultimate origin from the Epic of Gilgamesh and other epics of

the Sumerians circa 3,000 BC." Temple, *He Who Saw Everything: A Verse Translation of the Epic of Gilgamesh*, viii.

17. Humphrey Carpenter, *J. R. R. Tolkien: A Biography* (London: G. Allen & Unwin, 1978), 151.

18. Philip Zaleski and Carol Zaleski, *The Fellowship: The Literary Lives of the Inklings: J.R.R. Tolkien, C. S. Lewis, Owen Barfield, Charles Williams* (New York: Farrar, Straus and Giroux, 2015), 188.

19. J. R. R. Tolkien, *Tree and Leaf: Including Mythopoeia and the Homecoming of Beorhtnoth* (London: Harper Collins Publishers, 1988), 85.

20. Tolkien, *Tree and Leaf: Including Mythopoeia and the Homecoming of Beorhtnoth*, 86.

21. James Hillman, *Healing Fiction* (Dallas: Spring Publications, 1994), 17-18.

22. See Francisco Vaz da Silva, "The Invention of Fairy Tales," *The Journal of American folklore* 123, no. 490 (2010), https://doi.org/10.1353/jaf.2010.0001.

23. "Top Lifetime Grosses (Worldwide)," Box Office Mojo by IMDB Pro, updated March 5, 2023, accessed March 5, 2023, https://www.boxofficemojo.com/chart/top_lifetime_gross/?area=XWW. *Avengers: Endgame*, directed by Anthony Russo and Joe Russo holds the #2 spot in worldwide top lifetime grosses unadjusted for inflation, with *Star Wars: Episode VII—The Force Awakens* in #5, *Avengers: Infiinity War* directed by Joss Whedon in #6, and *The Avengers* directed by Joss Whedon in #10.

24. Burns, *Empire of Dreams: The Story of the Star Wars Trilogy*.

Acknowledgments

Writing may be a solitary endeavor, but I was never alone on this journey. Firstly, many thanks to my editor, Jessica Tepper, for her constancy in kind words and encouragement. With genuine appreciation, I acknowledge the cooperation of the Joseph Campbell Foundation for their permission to cite from his influential works, a contribution that significantly enhances the academic scope of this volume.

In the generous spirit of academic fellowship, I extend my deepest appreciation to my mentors, Rosie Dub, Jacqueline Yallop, Matthew Francis, and Brian Klug. They have willingly imparted their wisdom and shared their expertise, leading by example with their rigor and intellectual interests. I am profoundly indebted to them for their guidance. Special thanks to James MacGregor for the invaluable role he played in my professional journey.

To my students, past and present, especially Abdul Rahman Abid, Zain Assaf, Muaaz Dembinski, Ali Ahmar, Aesha Hussein, Tala Bibi, Gaebriel Olsen, and Rodolfo Muñoz Cárdenas, I offer my heartfelt thanks. Their inquisitive minds, insightful questions, and bright enthusiasm have been a constant source of motivation. They have contributed much to this process by challenging monomythic assumptions and inspiring new perspectives.

I echo Isaac Newton's sentiment, "If I have seen further it is by standing on the shoulders of Giants," and am much obliged to the scholars and storytellers whose works I have learned and benefited from. I genuinely value the inestimable resources provided by Georgetown University, Northwestern University, and DePaul University libraries, as well as the Internet Archives. The diligent librarians and the comprehensive collections have been an indispensable part of my research. These sanctuaries of knowledge not only provided the raw materials for this book but also offered a conducive atmosphere for contemplation and writing.

My sincere thanks go to my friends and family, whose ceaseless encouragement, shared wisdom, and constant cheer helped me maintain perspective during the many challenges that accompanied this venture. My special thanks to Zainab Khan for motivating me to stay the course, to Jackleen Salem for her support in heart and spirit, to Maryam Salem for her boundless curiosity in storytelling and story crafting, and to Salih Salem for his unflagging confidence in my work and the stimulating debates we had over all things MCU and SWCU.

I'm so thankful to my parents, Jusara Oldenberg and Salem M. Salem, who gave me the space and freedom to forge my own path.

And for Ibrahim N. Abusharif—I am grateful.

This book is truly a collective achievement. To everyone mentioned and not mentioned, thank you for being part of my journey.

Chapter 1

On Mythic Quests

An Introduction

"I could snap my fingers, and they would all cease to exist," Thanos says, ushering in the ultimate war between the super good and super bad in Marvel's mythopoeic film series, *The Avengers*. He's speaking about ending humankind as a punishment for ingratitude. But who is he, and why did audiences care enough to make the story of his demise (not to mention the hero collective that snapped him) in the *Avengers: Endgame* (2019) the highest grossing film in history worldwide? Taking after his Greek god namesake Thanatos, Thanos is a godlike creature of death, and he's fulfilling the mythic promise of evil that dates back to beginning times and certain origin stories relating to Satan's temptation of Adam and Eve. They didn't deserve heaven, and now their progeny doesn't deserve earth—a creation story with a villainously victorious finale, if not for the triumph of humanity. The superhero genre popularized by Marvel Studios taps into a long, rich mythological tradition establishing that myths continue to resonate with people today. But what is it about mythology that still fuels storytelling?

Since the earliest times, primal stories served as a wellspring for ancient wisdom from our forebears, providing an existential discourse on humanity's genesis, heritage, and destiny, laced with parables for right action. But it's more than a catalogue of cautionary tales of past events and prophesized futures. Akin to a primordial form of subliminal messaging, mythology utilizes archetypes to elicit spiritual or psychological responses, serving as a bridge to the unknown. Myths can be described literally as a story about gods with religious implications regarding creation or figuratively as a story with symbolic content drawn from the unseen to give deeper meaning to life. As sacred stories, they are absolutely true in some cultures, metaphorically true in others.

In an attempt to comprehend the full import of mythology, scholars have examined it under philology, anthropology, religion, sociology, philosophy, literature, ethnology, history, and theology.[1] For Max Muller, the corpus of inherited myths represents a corruption of language personifying abstract concepts. The heroes of legends reflect a primitive understanding of supernatural powers that eventually became deified in time. In James Frazer's anthropological study of myth and religion, *The Golden Bough*, he interprets the height of human intellectual achievement, science, as arising from primeval magic that evolved into religion which eventually distilled into its pure form—rational thought. Although his Darwinian assumptions about primitive man buckled under post-structuralist criticism, his thirteen volumes on myth and lore left an indelible intertextual impression on the literary world as well as the psychological, influencing the likes of Robert Graves, William Butler Yeats, T. S. Eliot, James Joyce, Ernest Hemingway, D. H. Lawrence, Sigmund Freud, and Carl Jung. It also birthed the myth and ritual school that became associated with the Cambridge Ritualists and influenced the greater field of comparative religion through Samuel Henry Hooke and Mircea Eliade and sociology through Emile Durkheim. Frazer controversially suggests that Jesus Christ represented an archetype of the resurrected god in a history of mythological examples that included Osiris, Adonis, Dionysus, and others.

For Durkheim, myths are not rarified embodiments of ancient concepts but a vehicle for moral values that continue to cement society. The allegories of mythology instruct individual behavior on social conformity. Carl Jung holds that myths were "the original revelations of the preconscious psyche" and the reflected dreams of a collective unconscious.[2] Ananda Coomaraswamy read metaphysical meaning into myths, while Western agnostics speculated that the Bible was another form of mythology as a revelation from God. Joseph Campbell gave myth the broadest definition, claiming that of the aforementioned examples, "Mythology is all of these." In an interview, he calls it "a metaphor for the experience of life."[3] According to Mircea Eliade, "Myths are the most general and effective means of awakening and maintaining consciousness of another world, a beyond, whether it be the divine world or the world of the Ancestors. This 'other world' represents a superhuman, 'transcendent' plane, the plane of absolute realities."[4] Myths constitute a paradigm for living life in the form of a sacred narrative.

Mythology dates back to the Paleolithic era of cave paintings, which according to some anthropological theories, show primitive man's relation to shamanic rituals. Over thousands of years, complex mythologies and religious systems developed around the world. The ancient civilizations of Mesopotamia, Egypt, India, and Greece were among the first to record their mythologies. Many other cultures, including those of the Romans, Canaanites, diverse groups across Europe, Anatolia, Asia, Africa, and the Pacific Islands, as well as Indigenous peoples such as the Aboriginal Australians, Native Americans, and South American Indigenous peoples also developed rich mythological traditions, often preserved and passed down through oral story-telling, art, ritual, and other forms of cultural expression. For early societies, myths represented truth about religion, science, and the world. With the passage of time, the transmutation of varied versions, and the eventual advent of secularized science, myth diverged and separated from certainty—socially relegated to a vestige of metaphor, symbol, or poetry. As soon as the late period of Greek civilization, Plato questions the misleading value of Homer and pits philosophy against poetry as fact against fiction.

Myths often feature a hero who represents an archetype of the exemplary person experiencing a transformative struggle. Campbell refers to him as a man of "self-achieved submission."[5] He is not necessarily a hero at the outset of his mythic quest but, in undertaking the struggles of the journey, becomes one by the end. As a representation of a sacred experience with a god-image, hero-myths have been studied for patterns since the nineteenth century. In 1871, Edward Taylor was the earliest anthropologist to uncover a common structure to many myths. He was followed by the works of Johann Georg van Hahn, Vladimir Propp, Karl Abraham, and Otto Rank. Joseph Campbell was not the first to locate a uniform mythic structure or theorize about it from a psychological perspective, but he would become the most popular.

In 1909, Karl Abraham undertook a Freudian interpretation of myth in *Dreams and Myths*. More prolifically, Otto Rank also interpreted myth from a Freudian perspective.[6] Freud's psychoanalysis of the myth Oedipus led to his theory of the "Oedipus Complex" surrounding a child's unconscious desires. Carl Jung, a former student of Freud's, also studied myth from a psychoanalytic perspective, drawing conclusions as to mythical representations of the individuation process. Gods and goddesses represented archetypal aspects of the Ego's relation to the Self. On the heels of such predecessors in psychoanalytical mythological thought, Joseph Campbell discovered a mythic structure that represents ego development and transformation as depicted by the archetype of a hero.

Taken collectively and reduced to its common elements, a hero travels the same universal journey in an epic pursuit of transformation—the "destiny of Everyman."[7] In *The Hero with a Thousand Faces*, Campbell labels this the "monomyth," maintaining that regardless of origin in the East or the West, there is the one constant relatable story that crosses time and geography.[8] Arguing from a psychological theoretical framework, he outlines a heroic journey for a universal mythic structure that purports to describe humanity's psychological (the rise and fall of the ego), metaphysical (the rise and fall of the soul), sociological (the rise and fall of nations), and cosmological (the rise and fall of humanity) exigencies. Whether Campbell was successful as a mythologist in his broad claims remains academically debatable, but his conception of a possible mythic structure to story has captured the imagination of writers searching for the illusive golden mean to the narrative form. Interest in Campbell's work garnered the avid attention of Hollywood, audiences, and readers, culminating in a six-hour documentary interview with Bill Moyers, hosted by George Lucas at his Skywalker Ranch, which was posthumously aired in 1988. This was followed by a companion book of the same title, *The Power of Myth*, that became a New York Times bestseller and remained so for 57 weeks.

George Lucas credits Campbell's monomyth for the mythopoesis of *Star Wars*, in which Lucas consciously set out to tell a story that draws on mythic motifs and its inherent structure. "I'm telling an old myth in a new way. That's how you pass down the meat and potatoes of your society."[9] He believes that "Myths help you to have your own hero's journey, find your individuality, find your place in the world, but hopefully remind you that you're part of a whole and that you must also be part of the community and think of the welfare of the community above the welfare of yourself."[10] He wasn't alone in his belief or the first. Contemporaneously with the publication of *The Hero with a Thousand Faces* and across the ocean, J.R.R. Tolkien popularized the term "mythopoeia" to reflect the kind of creative writing that purposefully incorporated myth-making into story, which he then epitomized in *The Lord of the Rings* series. Mythopoeia recognizes mythology as an ongoing endeavor of humanity, especially for storytellers, and not something exhumed from the ruins of any fallen ancient empire. Reinterpreting myth for modern times satisfies the human desire to feel that we are not alone and that others have struggled and overcome before us, regardless of whether those "others" were literal or metaphorical. The truth of the human experience remains.

While Tolkien's work has been canonized as the font of modern fantasy fiction, *Star Wars* later launched a new generation of mythopoesis in movies, many of which account for the highest grossing films of all time.[11] Writers have tried to capitalize on the secrets to myth-making success. Christopher Vogler provides the most succinct summation in *The Writer's Journey: Mythic Structure for Writers*.[12] But a close read of the monomyth reveals certain flaws that dates it as a product of antiquated androcentric views. While early in the text of *The Hero with a Thousand Faces*, Campbell argues that the journey is for both men and women, he later confesses that women need not concern themselves with becoming "pseudo-male." His chapter, "Woman as a Temptress," essentializes women to one sexist function. In addition, Campbell proposes a theory that he doesn't prove with a single all-encompassing myth, resorting instead to authorial fiat. He's known as a scholar in his field, but he doesn't reference or quote his peers, writing instead in a vacuum of his thoughts. He claims that the monomyth "conducts individuals through the ineluctable psychophysiological stages of transformation of a human lifetime" but doesn't explain how.[13] Finally, Campbell expounds a monomythic blueprint with seventeen steps but then concludes that not all steps are strictly necessary, and some may be repeated, begging the question of whether a structure exists after all.

Some of these flaws have been cured by Vogler's work, which was first published in 1998. Vogler reduces the journey to twelve necessary steps that a male or female character may embark upon, making the monomyth more accessible to storytellers and accomplishing what Campbell never could by providing complete examples of the mythic quest in story and establishing that a single narrative can encompass the entirety of a hero's journey to wide psychological satisfaction. Like Campbell, Vogler's proof depends not so much upon a mechanical formula of milestones, but upon Carl Jung's theory of archetypes and psychological development wherein a person (or character) achieves inner transformation by engaging in the steps of the hero's journey which inherently encapsulates the Ego's discovery of the Self. In essence, regardless of age, gender, ethnicity, or socio-economic background, human yearning touches everyone around the world, especially the desire to better oneself, which is the professed objective of the monomyth—to become heroic by finding one's true self.

Although Vogler intends the hero's journey to apply to men and women, he confesses in the third edition:

> The Hero's Journey is sometimes critiqued as a masculine theory, cooked up by men to enforce their dominance, and with little relevance to the unique and quite different journey of womanhood. There may be some masculine bias built into the description of the hero cycle since many of its theoreticians have been male, and I freely admit it: I'm a man and can't help seeing the world through the filter of my gender.[14]

By the fourth edition, however, he elides this confession, presumably no longer comfortable making proclamations of gender or assumptions of any journey upon women different to men, hinting at the tension between the totalizing force of homogeneity and the attraction of the infinite ends of heteronomy (a topic I explore in Chapter Six). Additionally, in recent years, Vogler's structure seems to have encountered an invisible impasse. Call-to-adventure stories are tired, which is not surprising considering that Hollywood has been chasing the *Star Wars* formula for at least 40 years. But this may also owe in some measure to the quest's recurring theme of adolescent development. Lucas calls it a story for kids. Campbell refers to it as the archetypal adventure of becoming a youth. The hero's adventure is so focused on developing and strengthening the ego that the hero has become a god of individualism. Religious studies scholar and mythographer, William Doty, observes:

One wonders . . . if the traditional hero model celebrated in America is still appropriate for adults. How can it be that so much of our mass entertainment (with its Cowboy or Vice Squad or John Rambo) is fixated at a teenage level of development? Campbell proposes that the hero "evolves as the culture evolves," but unfortunately, he did not show us what he meant by that remark, nor did he develop adequately a monomyth of the heroine such as Maureen Murdock has proposed, focused not upon conquest but upon human interrelationships.[15]

Doty argues for a "new heroicism," especially with regards to finding more heroines.[16]

The hero's journey's current wane of appeal results not necessarily from its androcentrism but from its fixation on teenage development, perpetually focused on reiterating only part of the story of individuation—that of the first half of life. What of the journey for the second half of life? Where are the midlife heroes? It's my contention that there's more to the archetypal arc. What is missing from the monomyth and consequent current mythopoeia is the heroine's journey, not because it's the perceived antithesis to the hero's journey, which it's not, but because it complements a lifelong experience that begins with the first half of life, coming of age, as expressed by a hero's journey and ends with the second half of life, coming of *middle* age, as conveyed in a heroine's journey. Baby boomers, Gen Xers, and even some Millennials that grew up on *Star Wars* desire stories featuring more mid-life heroes. A call to adventure speaks less to them than a call to home. But what does that call, a heroine's journey, entail?

Campbell didn't believe that the mythic quest applied to women, which raised questions about the universality of his monomyth. Feminist and Jungian scholars criticize Joseph Campbell for being androcentric and advocate for a description of the female experience in a separate heroic journey with its own archetypes and myths.[17] Maureen Murdock interviewed Campbell about the place for women in a hero's journey to which he said, "In the whole mythological tradition, the woman is there. All she has to do is realize that she's the place that people are trying to get to. When a woman realizes what her wonderful character is, she's not going to get messed up with the notion of being pseudo-male."[18] To categorically proclaim that in the entire mythological history spanning a multitude of cultures, women do nothing but exist is to deny many myths featuring goddess journeys, not to mention the actual experiences of women.[19] In *The Power of Myth*, Campbell reduces women to their biological function, arguing that their body dictates their development into women. Men on the other hand must choose to become men, which makes their journey more difficult and also heroic. Women are passive victims of their nature, while men have the inherent aptitude for greatness.[20]

Dissatisfied with Campbell's response to her query on the role of women in myth, Maureen Murdock, a post-Jungian psychologist with over twenty years of experience, eventually bucked Campbellian tradition and wrote *The Heroine's Journey, Woman's Quest for Wholeness*, which defines the patterns of behavior that arose from her many years of professional practice in helping women heal—patterns with Jungian underpinnings and mythic resonance. Murdock's stages of healing purports to describe the psychological growth process to maturity and coming to terms with one's life as already lived, what in literature is referred to as a *künstlerroman* versus the coming-of-age *bildungsroman*.

Joseph Campbell may be rescued from his patriarchal and gendered assumptions, but what will rescue him from postmodernism, which unseated the supremacy of universal theories from the modern age? By his own admission, *The Hero with a Thousand Faces* "presents in the form of one composite adventure the tales of a number of the world's symbolic carrier of the destiny of Everyman,"[21] marshalling contemporaneous Hegelian inspired idealism that influenced modernism. George Wilhelm Friedrich Hegel wrote a world history metanarrative as "the record of the spirit's efforts to attain knowledge of what it is in itself."[22] Unfortunately, his metanarrative was also Orientalist and Eurocentric because, as he notes, "[t]he Orientals do not know that the spirit or man as such are free in themselves. And because they do not know this, they are not themselves free. They only know that One is free; but for this very reason, such freedom is mere arbitrariness, savagery, and brutal passion. [. . .] The consciousness of freedom first awoke among the Greeks, and they were accordingly free."[23] The danger of grand narratives is that it purports to speak for all without hearing from all voices.

Postmodernism ushered in an era of "incredulity toward metanarratives,"[24] where a universal history no longer existed, only the local history—a reflection of the ongoing breakup with dominant culture and absolute truths. Canonized state stories could not and did not speak for everyone. But they weren't meant to. Rather, their function served cultural imperialism and the marginalization of the other, creating binaries that would lead to artificial divisions such as West versus non-West, civilized versus savage, white versus black, the colonizer versus the colonized, and the Occident versus the Orient, while privileging the former over the latter, respectively. According to Edward Said, orientalism institutionalizes Eurocentric approaches to the Orient "by making statements about it, authorizing views of it, describing it, by teaching it, settling it, ruling over it: in short, Orientalism [i]s a Western style for dominating, restructuring, and having authority over the Orient."[25] Postmodernism further challenges the hegemonic truths of science, which is legitimized by rationality, a social construct of the phallocratic kind. And to the extent that there is no truth, there is no God, concluding a secular

forethought that began with a literal construction and willful misinterpreta-
tion of Nietzsche's proclamation that "God is dead."

Without grand histories, what can be known are local histories and relative
truths. Deconstruction upends dichotomous, privileged approaches in order
to recognize others and their histories. For that purpose, postcolonial theory
developed to overthrow Western imperialism and its colonial incursions into
indigenous history, discourse, culture, society, philosophy, religion, education, law, and literature. However, the postmodern skepticism for universal
truth is seen as appealing to a liberalized, secularized Western collective from
which it sprung and embodying what it criticizes—a grand narrative: there are
no universal truths except for this one about universal truths. Decoloniality
then turns postmodernism on itself as nothing more than a provincial epis-
teme of the global north, allowing for the introduction of transmodernism—a
global south theory resuscitating a universality of truth from the pluriversal
perspective.

This book reviews the existing theoretical framework for the monomyth
in the light of post-Jungian psychology from a transmodern perspective, and
the conceptual framework of the monomyth is re-examined for mythopoesis
through a hermeneutical approach. In the context of discussing mythology,
it's noteworthy that hermeneutics derives from the Greek god Hermes, the
great mediator of interpretation for the soul of the divine, "the guide and the
giver of good."[26] James Hillman employs hermeneutics in depth psychology:

> [Hermes]is himself a healing fiction, a God. And Hermes heals by convincing
> us of that fiction of interpretation, making it work, so that the interpreter hits
> just on the word which opens the way. But if Hermes is to function properly as
> a guide of souls we must have some material for him to turn into a message.
> [. . .] There must be something to move across the threshold and exchange,
> translate into an insight. He appears in the interpretive act, his gift is the insight.
> One recognizes where he has been by the mound of stones erected to mark his
> intervention. And these boundary stones go on being erected in the psyche as
> part of its soul history [. . .] after a bit of deft hermeneutical work has been done
> on a dream or a story.[27]

A hermeneutical approach makes unconscious material available to conscious
interpretation.

For purposes of this study, the terms "hero" and "heroine" are unsexed, not
referring to man and woman. Rather, I take the hero's journey to represent the
bildungsroman quest for adulthood, while the heroine's journey represents
the *künstlerroman* quest for maturation. Originally, the eighteenth-century
term bildungsroman derived from the German word *bildung,* meaning education and *roman*, meaning novel and represented German literature where a

male protagonist comes of age, but has, in the intervening centuries, enveloped the broader genre of the transition into adulthood irrespective of gender or origin. Professor of English and Comparative Literature, Marianne Hirsch defines it as "novel[s] of formation" because it encompasses the "novel of development, of education, apprenticeship, initiation, youth [. . .] suggesting both the process of education that is depicted in these novels and the product that takes shape (or form) as it grows out of itself and in response to external factors."[28] The künstlerroman, meaning the artist's novel, reflects the semi-autobiographical story of an artist, who presumably came of an age in a bildungsroman and matures into an aspirant searching for the metaphysical by creative expression, as someone who, according to Evy Varsamopoulou, "seeks another world and finds it, not in religion, but in art, which he pursues with a religious devotion. [. . .] Hence the attraction to what is otherworldly: fairies, magic, infinity, spirituality, the sublime."[29] Roberta White defines the modern künstlerroman as "the story of an artist's intellectual and emotional growth; usually it describes an inward journey leading to a discovery of the artist's vocation."[30] The artist may be a painter, poet, musician, novelist, or anyone engaged in a creative pursuit. Professor Maurice Beebe, author of *Ivory Towers and Sacred Founts*, in discussing the künstlerroman as a portrait-of-the-artist type novel wherein the artist is the hero, argues that:

> It should be understood that I am using the term "artist" to mean anyone capable of creating works of art, whether literary, musical, or visual. In fact, actual production is not a requirement for the artist-hero, for some of the characters I discuss are only potential artists, and a few are not identified as artists at all, though they are obviously surrogates for their authors.[31]

From its early conception in modern psychology, founder of individual psychology and member of the Vienna Circle along with Sigmund Freud and Carl Jung, Alfred Adler, proposes that "masculine protest" is a "compensation for a feeling of inferiority."[32] He defines "masculine" and "feminine" not so much as intrinsic, genetic psychic functions but ones made so by culture.

> The deep-rooted feeling that permeates the folk-soul and which has always awakened the interest of poets and thinkers, that evaluation and symbolizing of types of phenomena as "masculine" and "feminine," although seemingly arbitrary and yet coinciding with our social life, impresses itself early upon the infant mind. Thus the child, with occasional variations, regards the following as masculine: strength, greatness, riches, knowledge, victory, coarseness, cruelty, violence and activity as such, their opposites being feminine.[33]

Perhaps Freud can be credited with concretizing a genetic function of the masculine energies when he claimed that boys experience castration anxiety of being dispossessed of their biological male essence—the phallus—while girls suffer from penis envy for not having one (overlooking an androcentric bias inherent in his theory of the "phallic stage" in psychosexual development). Carl Jung ascribed a feminine aspect to men's psyches and a masculine aspect to women's psyche. Post-Jungian psychologists broadened this theory to locate a masculine and feminine energy in every psyche irrespective of sex. Queer theory scholar Judith Butler takes this a step further by arguing that gender and sex are social constructs not defined by bodily facticity. Gender is not something that one is, it is something one does—a "doing" rather than a "being."[34] Whereas gender norms of masculine and feminine may have historically been viewed from a structuralist, binary perspective, Butler takes a post-structuralist view to deconstruct and subvert gender norms. However, Butler's presumption that gender is binary—which it can be to the extent that anyone takes a strict structuralist view that a person is either masculine or feminine and never both—overlooks the literature on bisexuality and androgyny. Adler points to a psychic structure as "compensatory" in a scheme of superiority versus inferiority[35]—in the context of this study, a superior ego dominating an inferiorized soul—a scheme which a modern patriarchal society later reduces and tags to an assumption of masculine superiority dominating a feminine inferiority contributing to a host of harmful social implications subsequently challenged by discourses on politics of difference and disrupted by feminism and post-feminisms. For Adler, "to think that abstract opposites reflect reality is to think neurotically, since all antitheses ultimately refer to the power construct of superior/inferior embodied in society as male and female."[36] Jung also suggests a compensatory scheme between consciousness, which he views as masculine, and the unconscious, which he views as feminine. "[T]he unconscious does not simply act *contrary* to the conscious mind but *modifies* it more in the manner of an opponent or partner."[37] For Hillman, a binary assumption "severs the ambivalence" inherent in "psychic hermaphroditism" which "holds juxtapositions without feeling them as oppositions," while psychotherapy restores the ambivalence.[38]

Thus, we are disposed to antithetical modes of thinking in balancing out feelings of inferiority and security, which act as "guiding fictions."[39] While oppositions between conscious and the unconscious, masculine and feminine, positive and negative present illustrative fictions, they reveal a severance from the ambivalent nature of the psyche which seeks healing. The mind is not binary. It can simultaneously host feminine and masculine energies however they may be defined in current cultural contexts. They are compensatory in the sense that the feminine aspect tempers the masculine aspect and the masculine aspect tempers the feminine. And when both are equally tempered any difference between them disappears and the psyche achieves the harmony it longs for. I recognize that the terms "masculine" and "feminine" are fraught with a binary implication that has been disempowering in a patriarchal society. I engage these terms with full knowledge of their limitations and by no means suggest a monolithic understanding of "masculine" or "feminine." In the context of mythopoesis, a myth-maker makes use of these cultural motifs to draw out relatable metaphors for lived experiences. These archetypes are fluidly defined by the imagination and by related social markers from different centuries or societies, as the case may be. Culturally, historically, and mythologically, this grappling has been reified in the paradigm of a superior masculine versus an inferior feminine and exemplified in Eros and Psyche, *Jane Eyre*, and *Titanic*. It would be reductive to sterilize these stories from the context of their creation out of an abundance of caution to side-step any post-feminist critique based on gender theory. Where Butler argues that gender is in *doing* rather than *being*, she makes the same totalizing assumption that she criticizes just from the other end of the spectrum, engaging in a binarism between what one *is* and what one *does*. The question is, why can't gender be both? The monomyth as rebooted assumes that gender is in doing *and* in being, the former being the hero's journey and the latter the heroine's.

Psychotherapy presents one manner of working with the intrapsychic life of maleness and femaleness, while mythopoesis presents another. Consequently, scholars press for a descent to the goddess, a run with the wolves, a dance with the flames, a return to the goddess, a meeting with the great mother, an encounter with the soul, an awakening of the woman, an understanding of the soul's code, and a remythologizing of life.[40] In *Descent to the Goddess*, Sylvia Brinton Perera argues that:

> The patriarchal ego of both men and women, to earn its instinct-disciplining, striving, progressive, and heroic stance, has fled from the full scale awe of the goddess. Or it has tried to slay her, or at least to dismember and thus depotentiate her. But it is towards her—and especially towards her culturally repressed aspects, those chthonic and chaotic, ineluctable depths—that the new individuating, yin-yang balanced ego must return to find its matrix and the embodied and flexible strength to be active and vulnerable, to stand its own ground and still to be empathetically related to others.[41]

In *Psychotherapy Grounded in the Feminine Principle*, Barbara Stevens Sullivan explains that:

> Myths or fairy tales depict the ways the masculine or feminine principles are incomplete in themselves, needing a connection to the other principle. The Iliad, for example, begins with the theft of the Feminine (Helen) from Greece by Troy. The enraged Greek warriors wait endlessly on the beach for favorable winds to take them to Troy. At last Agamemnon sacrifices his daughter,

Iphigenia, to the gods to win the winds' cooperation. In order to undertake this masculine task of making war the men must absolutely sever their connection to the Feminine. Although this approach begins the tale that ends in a Greek victory, the tremendous problems stemming from pure masculinity unrelieved by any feminine elements are dealt with in a number of related mythic sagas. When Agamemnon returns from Troy the Feminine takes revenge on him in the person of his wife, Iphigenia's mother, who murders him for his heartlessly goal-oriented behavior.[42]

For Hillman, "Ego consciousness as we used to know it no longer reflects reality. The ego has become a delusional system."[43] Regardless of placement on any preconceived gender spectrum, anyone can become a "hero" or "hero-ine" as a function of psychological growth and maturation.

The hero and heroine's journey taken together in the light of post-Campbellian mythography and post-Jungian psychology, represent the journey of a life—the monomyth rebooted at last. In the beginning, there's a desperate urge to separate from the unconscious and become an individual. As a person matures, the desire for wholeness supersedes and drives them back to a reunion with the unconscious. On a psychological level, the masculine and feminine aspects are balanced. *The Monomyth Reboot* re-examines the psychological framework to provide a unified theory of the hero and heroine journeys that expresses a more inclusive vision of the monomyth as supported by post-Jungian concepts and evidenced across time and genre in the myth of Eros and Psyche, the novel of *Jane Eyre*, and the film *Titanic*. Chapter 2, "Understanding the Monomyth," presents the monomyth as originally intended from Campbell's perspective, reflecting each one of his seventeen steps with focused commentary. Conceptually, he reduces mythology to usable building blocks available to everyone for living their best lives or overcoming trials or sending one's characters on journeys of transformation. But on closer inspection, the way in which he describes some of those fundamental components leaves out a measure of scholarly rigor and leans into cultural assumptions and inherent biases.

To address these concerns, I undertake a two-pronged approach. First, in Chapter 3, I examine the monomyth from the Jungian and post-Jungian psychological perspective, giving it the treatment Campbell alluded to but never defined. Without attempting to be exhaustive to the field, I concentrate on the correlation between the psychoanalytic theory of individuation and the underpinnings of the monomyth. Second, once Campbell's theory finds proper footing in psychology, it's possible to consider it for purposes of mythopoesis. Yet certain components of his theory remain fraught with outmoded cultural views in relation to various members of the marginalized. To cure this and to reflect the process of individuation in the monomyth, I divide it into two main journeys of life, coming of age and coming of middle age. In story, the hero and heroine's journey reflect these life experiences, respectively; but from a creative writing perspective, they can be told simultaneously for a richer, more comprehensive, intellectually stimulating text-based or audio-visual engagement, as reflected in works such as Eros and Psyche, *Jane Eyre*, and *Titanic*. Chapter 4 delves into Christopher Vogler's abridged version of the monomyth in *The Writer's Journey*, which has become synonymous with the hero's journey. He effectively deletes and reassembles the stages in an attempt to modernize the theory for current writers. Where Campbell reduced mythology to seventeen steps, Vogler further reduces it to twelve, without reflection upon the consequences. He takes liberties with the theory with less scholarly rigor than Campbell. Because I map the hero's journey against the process of individuation, I show how this serendipitous abridgement is successful. Historically, before Vogler or Campbell, writers have subconsciously picked up on the psychic story pattern.

To complete the revisioning of the monomyth, Chapter 5 continues the story of individuation in midlife by investigating the heroine's journey from Maureen Murdock's psychoanalytic perspective. Drawing inspiration from Campbell, she consolidates narratives of patient experiences to posit nine steps a woman undergoes to achieve wholeness. To degender and scale this for mythopoesis, I extrapolate from Murdock's theory and expound on the heroine's journey in twelve steps, referencing the same three examples also used for the hero's journey. Before uniting the hero and heroine's journeys, Chapter 6 considers the postmodern critique of the monomyth with a view towards transmodernism. How can a "grand theory" overcome relativistic deconstructionism? I begin with an overview of modernism and postmodernism to situate Joseph Campbell in critical theory in which his work may have been reductively dismissed as an artifact of modernism when he was actually more of a traditionalist. Chapter 7 joins together the hero and heroine's journey as reimagined into a singular relevant reflection of the monomyth, with examples from the global south along with final thoughts on the movie that brought us here as a prime illustration of the monomyth rebooted. This book establishes that while the monomyth may have fallen into disfavor as a result of arcane, universalistic views that privileges an androcentric perspective, the concept, as amended, retains continuing relevance to storytellers seeking to make outer sense of an inner world.

NOTES

1. William G. Doty, *Mythography: The Study of Myths and Rituals*, 2nd ed. (Tuscaloosa: University of Alabama Press, 2000), xiii. While it may be beyond the scope

of this monograph to delve into every theoretical methodology of mythography, it is worth noting that mythography can be approached from sociological, anthropological, linguistic, feminist, theosophical, and other psychological perspectives. For sociological studies on mythography see Bronislaw Malinowski and Robert Redfield, *Magic, Science and Religion, and Other Essays* (Boston: Beacon Press, 1948); Emile Durkheim, *The Elementary Forms of Religious Life*, trans. Karen E. Fields (New York: Free Press, 1995). For an anthropological view on myth and ritual see Victor W. Turner, *The Ritual Process: Structure and Anti-Structure* (Chicago: Aldine Pub. Co., 1969). For a linguistic perspective, see Roland Barthes and Stephen Heath, *Image, Music, Text* (New York: Hill and Wang, 1977). For a structuralist view, see Claude Lévi-Strauss, *Myth and Meaning* (Toronto, Buffalo: University of Toronto Press, 1978); Claude Lévi-Strauss, *The Naked Man* (New York: Harper & Row, 1981). For a broadly defined feminist perspective, Carol Pearson and Katherine Pope, *The Female Hero in American and British Literature* (New York: Bowker, 1981); Carol Pearson, *Persephone Rising: Awakening the Heroine Within* (New York: HarperElixir, 2015); Carolyne Larrington, *The Feminist Companion to Mythology* (London: Pandora Press, 1992). For queer theory, see K. J. Dover, *Greek Homosexuality* (London: Duckworth, 1978); Zairong Xiang, *Queer Ancient Ways: A Decolonial Exploration* (Santa Barbara: Punctum Books, 2018). For a theosophical consideration, see Mircea Eliade, *Cosmos and History: The Myth of the Eternal Return* (New York: Harper, 1959). For the Freudian perspective, see Sigmund Freud, *Totem and Taboo: Resemblances between the Psychic Lives of Savages and Neurotics*, trans. A. A. Brill (New York: Moffat, Yard and Company, 1918); Otto Rank, *The Myth of the Birth of the Hero: A Psychological Interpretation of Mythology*, trans. F. Robbins and Smith Ely Jelliffe (New York: The Journal of Nervous and Mental Disease Publishing Company, 1914).

2. C. G. Jung, "The Archetypes and the Collective Unconscious," in *The Collected Works of C. G. Jung, Volume 9, Part 1*, ed. Herbert Read et al. (2nd, Princeton: Princeton University Press, 1980).

3. Burns, *Star Wars: The Legacy Revealed.*

4. Mircea Eliade, *Myth and Reality* (New York: Harper & Row, 1963), 139.

5. Joseph Campbell, *The Hero With a Thousand Faces*, 2nd ed. (Princeton: Princeton University Press, 1968), 10.

6. See Karl Abraham, *Dreams and Myths: A Study in Race Psychology*, trans. William A. White (New York: The Journal of Nervous and Mental Disease Publishing Company, 1913); Rank, *The Myth of the Birth of the Hero: A Psychological Interpretation of Mythology.*

7. Joseph Campbell, *The Hero with a Thousand Faces* (Novato: New World Library, 2008), 28. All quotes from Joseph Campbell's *The Hero with a Thousand Faces.* Copyright © Joseph Campbell Foundation (jcf.org) 2008. Used with permission.

8. Campbell, *Hero*, 30.

9. *The Mythology of Star Wars with George Lucas and Bill Moyers.* Films On Demand. 1999. Accessed December 24, 2020. https://fod.infobase.com/PortalPlaylists .aspx?wID=103525&xtid=9102. See also, The New York Times Book Review Editor, D.J.R. Bruckner's interview with Joseph Campbell, "Joseph Campbell: 70 Years

of Making Connections," December 18, 1983. https://nyti.ms/3piHBOY accessed December 24, 2020.

10. *The Mythology of Star Wars with George Lucas and Bill Moyers*. Films On Demand. 1999. Accessed December 24, 2020. https://fod.infobase.com/PortalPlaylists .aspx?wID=103525&xtid=9102.

11. See Dimitra Fimi, "Later Fantasy Fiction: Tolkien's Legacy," in *A Companion to J. R. R. Tolkien*, ed. Stuart D. Lee (Malden: Wiley Blackwell, 2014); Christopher Vogler, *The Writer's Journey: Mythic Structure for Writers*, 3rd ed. (Studio City: Michael Wiese Productions, 2007), 371–72.

12. Vogler, *Writer's Journey*.

13. Joseph Campbell, The Inner Reaches of Outer Space: Metaphor as Myth and as Religion (Novato: New World Library, 2002), xiii.

14. Vogler, *Writer's Journey*, xxi.

15. William G. Doty, "Joseph Campbell's Myth and/versus Religion," *Soundings: An Interdisciplinary Journal* 79, no. 3–4 (1996): 436; William G. Doty, "Joseph Campbell's Myth 'and/versus' Religion," *Soundings: An Interdisciplinary Journal* 79, no. 3/4 (1996).

16. Doty, "Joseph Campbell's Myth 'and/versus' Religion," 437.

17. *See* Clarissa Pinkola Estés, *Women Who Run with the Wolves: Myths and Stories of the Wild Woman Archetype* (New York: Ballantine Books, 1992); Jean Shinoda Bolen, *Goddesses in Everywoman: Powerful Archetypes in Women's Lives*, 1st Quill ed. (New York: Quill, 2004); Maureen Murdock, *The Heroine's Journey: Woman's Quest for Wholeness* (Boston, New York: Shambhala, 1990); Annis Pratt, *Archetypal Patterns in Women's Fiction* (Bloomington: Indiana University Press, 1981); Pearson and Pope, *The Female Hero in American and British Literature*; Irene Claremont de Castillejo, *Knowing Woman: A Feminine Psychology* (New York: Putnam, 1973); Ann Belford Ulanov, *The Feminine in Jungian Psychology and in Christian Theology* (Evanston: Northwestern University Press, 1971).

18. Murdock, 2.

19. See Maria Tatar, *The Heroine with 1001 Faces* (New York: Liveright Publishing Corporation, 2021).

20. Joseph Campbell and Bill D. Moyers, *The Power of Myth* (New York: Doubleday, 1988), 103.

21. Campbell, *The Hero with a Thousand Faces*, 28. All quotes from Joseph Campbell's *The Hero with a Thousand Faces* Copyright © Joseph Campbell Foundation (jcf.org) 2008. Used with permission.

22. Georg Wilhelm Friedrich Hegel and Johannes Hoffmeister, *Lectures on the Philosophy of World History: Introduction, Reason in History* (Cambridge, New York: Cambridge University Press, 1975), 54.

23. Ibid.

24. Jean-François Lyotard, *The Postmodern Condition: A Report on Knowledge* (Minneapolis: University of Minnesota Press, 1984), xxiv.

25. Edward W. Said, *Orientalism* (New York: Vintage Books, 1979), 3.

26. Edith Hamilton, *Mythology* (repr. Boston: Back Bay Books, 1998), 144.

27. Hillman, *Healing Fiction*, 30.

28. Marianne Hirsch, "The Novel of Formation as Genre: Between Great Expectations and Lost Illusions in Studies in the Novel," *Genre* 12, no. 3 (1979): 295.

29. Evy Varsamopoulou, *The Poetics of the Kunstlerinroman and the Aesthetics of the Sublime* (Aldershot; Burlington: Ashgate, 2002), xii. Varsamopoulou also discusses the autobiographical nature of the *Künstlerroman*.

30. Roberta White, *A Studio of One's Own: Fictional Women Painters and the Art of Fiction* (Madison: Fairleigh Dickinson University Press, 2005), 13.

31. Maurice Beebe, *Ivory Towers and Sacred Founts: The Artist as Hero in Fiction from Goethe to Joyce* (New York: New York University Press, 1964), v.

32. Alfred Adler, *The Practice and Theory of Individual Psychology*, trans. Paul Radin, 2nd ed. (New York, London: Harcourt, K. Paul, Trench, Trubner & Co. Ltd., 1955), 117.

33. Adler, *The Practice and Theory of Individual Psychology*, 21.

34. Judith Butler, *Gender Trouble: Feminism and the Subversion of Identity* (New York: Routledge, 1990), 25. Quotations added for emphasis.

35. Adler, *The Practice and Theory of Individual Psychology*, 37.

36. Hillman, *Healing Fiction*, 100.

37. C. G. Jung, *Psychology and Alchemy*, 2d ed., Collected Works, (Princeton: Princeton University Press, 1968), 50–51.

38. Hillman, *Healing Fiction*, 102.

39. Hillman, *Healing Fiction*, 100.

40. See Sylvia Brinton Perera, *Descent to the Goddess: A Way of Initiation for Women* (Toronto: Inner City Books, 1981); Estés, *Women Who Run with the Wolves: Myths and Stories of the Wild Woman Archetype*; Marion Woodman and Elinor Dickson, *Dancing in the Flames: The Dark Goddess in the Transformation of Consciousness* (Boston: Shambhala, 1996). Bolen, *Goddesses in Everywoman: Powerful Archetypes in Women's Lives*; Edward C. Whitmont, *Return of the Goddess* (New York: Crossroad, 1982); Barbara Hannah, *Encounters with the Soul: Active Imagination as Developed by C.G. Jung* (Wilmette: Chiron Publications, 2001); Nancy Qualls-Corbett, *Awakening Woman: Dreams and Individuation* (Toronto: Inner City Books, 2002); James Hillman, *The Soul's Code: In Search of Character and Calling* (New York: Ballantine Books, 2017); Ulanov, *The Feminine in Jungian Psychology and in Christian Theology*.

41. Perera, *Descent to the Goddess: A Way of Initiation for Women*, 7.

42. Ulanov, *The Feminine in Jungian Psychology and in Christian Theology*, 19.

43. Hillman, *Healing Fiction*, 110.

Chapter 2

On the Monomyth

Understanding the Seventeen Steps

Mythology provides the inherited rites of passage through the perils of life where the heroes have tread before, delivering the symbols necessary to move the soul forward and allow the human spirit to transcend. For Joseph Campbell, the power of myth derives from the spontaneous discharge of a macrocosmic collective unconscious and the microcosmic psyche for the purpose of simultaneously coming to the center of ourselves and also being at one with the world. Thus, the hero-with-a-thousand-faces embarks on a journey of separation, initiation, and return that Campbell details in seventeen stages. To prove his claim of the existence of a single universal myth, Campbell sets forth numerous disparate examples, thin-sliced from across cultures, and then unapologetically places the onus of a complete proof on the reader.

> In the above section, and throughout the following pages, I have made no attempt to exhaust the evidence. To have done so . . . would have enlarged my chapters prodigiously without making the main line of the monomyth any clearer. Instead, I am giving in each section a few striking examples from a number of widely scattered, representative traditions. . . . Should [the reader] wish to prove whether all might have been cited for every section of the monomyth, he need only turn to some of the source volumes enumerated in the footnotes and ramble through a few of the multitude of tales.[1]

The monomythic hero begins his journey with a Call to Adventure wherein the hero is called to live or die, to awaken or come of age. This call may be a result of a blunder that rippled from the deep, the sudden unveiling of a new world, or a paradigm shift that moves the hero away from an outgrown way of life into change. The call is often brought by a herald, a destiny carrier in the form of a ghastly creature who creates a crisis by his appearance as a rejected or denied force of the physical or psychological realm. The call beckons from a dark forest, an overgrown tree, or a gurgling stream—some symbol of the Navel of the World—into the zone of unknown.

Campbell draws from the example of the Brothers Grimm Frog King fairy tale, where a bored princess wanders into a shadowy woods playing with a golden ball that falls into a well. A frog hears her cries and agrees to help her retrieve it in exchange for her love and companionship. The princess consents but then promptly forgets all about him as she walks off with her prized possession. Undeterred, the frog follows her home and demands his due, which her father forces her to comply with although she finds the frog odious. The frog shares her food but when he tries to share her bed, she angrily flings him against the wall. Then he suddenly morphs into a beautiful prince, set free from a curse by her actions whom she promptly marries. He then whisks her off to his castle the next day.

The frog heralds change for the princess, despite her repeated refusal to accept any. For Campbell, this evidences a call to adventure, although the princess hero is of questionable character who has transformation thrust upon her rather than arise from within her. She refuses to keep her promise and then tries to kill the promisee, for which she is repaid by the appearance of the most handsome husband prospect. Hardly the behavior of an admirable hero; the reward for her murderous intent is a happily-ever-after outcome. Campbell doesn't account for her problematic attitude except that the frog may represent the adamant call of the unconscious and the princess's response its egotistical rejection. If that's the case, Campbell would have served his theory better by placing this example under the guise of the next step, Refusal of the Call.

The true Call to Adventure in this fairy tale happens to the frog, for whom the story is actually named and whose water world changes when a ball ripples into it—the blunder that Campbell refers to. This, along with the sound of cries, awakens him literally and, as Campbell would argue, metaphorically. The golden globe crashing into his still waters represents the call of his unconscious to become Self-aware. The princess, a reflection of *his* ego, offers him all possible manner of worldly gains, her clothes, jewelry, and golden crown. But he wants something more, something deeper; he demands her friendship. Additionally, the princess heralds the call for she is the person of loathly character anticipated by Campbell at this stage.

After the frog helps her and she reneges, he chases after her. He is aided, almost supernaturally, by the insertion of the king demanding she honor her commitment. It's only after the princess tries to kill her unwelcome guest that the amphibian emerges in his true human form. This again reflects the antagonism between an imbalanced Ego and the calls of a higher Self; the frog has to submit to the trial because returning to an aquatic life, submerged, unaware, and alone is no longer an option. Ultimately, the frog symbolizes the Campbellian hero—a prince bewitched and abandoned in the woods in animal form when an auriferous orb splashes into his domain calling him to an adventure that ultimately transforms him into a fair husband and the king he was destined to be.

Campbell also references King Arthur's pursuit of a hare into the forest whereupon he finds a fountain. Taking a break from the chase, King Arthur falls into deep contemplation, which is interrupted by the appearance of a great beast whose consumption of water silences his very noisy belly, arresting the king's attention. Although this scene portends the Quest for the Holy Grail, this is not King Arthur's quest. And, in fact, the Questing Beast does not appear to King Arthur at the beginning of his journey as a Call to Adventure but more as a herald of his future demise. At this point in the legend, King Arthur has already claimed the sword in the stone, embarked upon many battles and trials, and received Excalibur. He feels guilty of the sin of sleeping with his sister, which gives him a nightmare of the child she will bear that will destroy him. He tries to shake the remnants of that haunting dream by hunting a hare that he runs down to death. He also kills his own horse, symbolic of soul, in doing so. Therefore, he slays his soul in chasing his heart. What's left is for his future monster-son to claim him. While the Questing Beast is a case of a hideous creature that lives in the water of a valley, it's an inapposite example of this stage of the journey.

Campbell cites the fable of the Arapaho girl who chases a porcupine up a continually growing cottonwood tree into a heavenly realm. In some iterations of this tale, the Arapaho girl fancies marrying the moon, who takes shape as the quilled force of nature to entice her to follow him, whereupon he reveals himself as a beautiful Moon-man. They marry and have a Moon-child. Thus, the porcupine's appeal, according to Campbell, "signifies that destiny has summoned the hero and transferred his spiritual center of gravity from within the pale of his society to a zone unknown."[2]

Finally, Campbell uses the example of Buddha, who was born the son of a king under a prophecy that he'd either become a Buddha or a king. His father did everything in his power to keep his son attracted to worldly pleasures and the future that royalty holds particularly by shielding him from the ills of society. But after meeting with a dead man, a sick man, an old man, and a monk, Buddha responds to his deep yearning to withdraw from the world and engage in an adventure of a different sort.

In concluding, Campbell hastily adds the arrival of Theseus to Athens to eventually slay Minotaur and Odysseus's delayed return home as a result of Poseidon's wrath and punishment, wedging in the latter as a foregone conclusion although Odysseus had already responded to the call of adventure to war years before. Relying on these curious and at times dubious exemplifications,

Campbell concludes that the invitation into the unknown may be reflected "as a distant land, a forest, a kingdom underground, beneath the waves, or above the sky, a secret island, lofty mountain top, or profound dream state; but it is always a place of fluid and polymorphous beings, unimaginable torments, superhuman deeds, and impossible delight."[3] He then famously invites readers to come to their conclusion regarding the certainty of a monomythic structure, which he assumes they invariably will.

The next stage is a Refusal of the Call to adventure where the hero expresses reluctance to abandon his home or his comfortable way of life. Those who absolutely refuse the call are doomed to suffer repeated calamity. Campbell devotes considerable attention to refusals in which the hero failed to ultimately complete a monomythic journey, examples that hardly serve his overarching argument of one quest for all. For example, Minos wishes to become king of Crete and asks Poseidon for a sign of his authority. Poseidon presents him a sacred bull to be sacrificed in the god's honor. But King Minos refuses his call to duty and lets the bull live. In retaliation, Poseidon curses King Minos's wife to fall in love with and mate the bull, resulting in the birth of a monstrous half-human, half-bull Minotaur, which the king entraps in a labyrinth. The failure to accept the divine call devolves into the king's source of terror, until later slayed by Theseus.

Daphne also refuses the call of Amor, who shoots her and Apollo with his arrows. She flees from Apollo's amorous pursuits, begging her father to transform her into a laurel tree rather than be captured by love. Irreconciled refusal also applies to the Persian city whose people are enstoned for the refusal of the call of God. It applies to Lot's wife who transforms into a pillar of salt for her transgression. It applies to Sleeping Beauty and her world that fell asleep by spell until awoken by a prince. It applies to Brunhild, whose father and god punishes her for refusing to marry by putting her into a magical sleep. The final instance Campbell gives is that of Prince Kamar al-Zaman, who refuses his father's repeated requests to marry and submits to a tower prison. A similar refusal is given by Princess Budur halfway around the world, and a similar fate befalls her. Campbell marches his examples along an endless parade of refusals imposed on the hero in the form of punishments. From a psychological perspective, this experience reflects a reluctance to give up the sanctity of one's ego. Campbell justifies these cases as a preemptive setup for the next step. "[A] deliberate, terrific refusal to respond to anything but the deepest [. . .] answer to the as yet unknown demand of some waiting void within: a kind of total strike [. . .] as a result of which some power of transformation carries the problem to a plane of new magnitudes, where it is [. . .] resolved."[4] For Campbell, the refusal is more of a life-negating spell that requires supernatural force to overcome, in the absence of which doom and destruction awaits. However, mythology is rife with refusals defeated by a lesser power of resistance. Campbell's description restricts the understanding of a refusal to a smaller, more adamant subset of a greater group.

The third stage of the monomyth is Supernatural Aid from which the hero receives help in surmounting his misgivings to the call through the assistance of a mentor with advice and amulets, representing a benevolent force of destiny and protection descending from the cosmos. Supernatural Aid triggers the hero to trust in the powers of the unconscious. To prove this step, Campbell offers several examples including that of Kyazimba, a member of an East African tribe who searches long and far for the land where the sun rises. Falling short, he is aided by the appearance of a crone who magically transports him to the zenith of the celestial sphere, where they meet with a chieftain from whom she requests help on behalf of Kyazimba. The leader blesses Kyazimba who then returns home and lives a prosperous life. The Indigenous peoples of the American Southwest have a folktale about the Spider Woman, another crone with supernatural abilities helping children who have fallen into a subterranean cave by giving them a charmed feather to protect them from their enemies. European fairy tales feature fairy godmothers or legends of saints. The Virgin figure intercedes for mercy. Dante is saved by Beatrice and the Virgin. Faust in various iterations is aided by Gretchen, Helen of Troy, and the Virgin. Theseus enters the labyrinth with the help of the thread of Ariadne. The supernatural helper may also be male in the form of a wizard, shepherd, hermit, teacher, guide, or stranger often seen in the figures of the Greek god Hermes, the Roman god Mercury, the Egyptian god Thoth, and in the Christian Holy Ghost. Reverting back to the story of the Persian prince refusing to marry, Kamar Al-Zaman is aided by the meddling of two Jinn who contrive to bring together the two most beautiful people on earth, even if against their wills—representing a form of supernatural aid from the unconscious. In the absence of a figure, the course of history or mother nature steps in to carry the hero serendipitously forward.

The next stage is the Crossing of the First Threshold where the hero meets with a watchman at the gate of magnified power, a potentially dangerous figure who may question his authority to pass or jealously guard the path into the unknown, depicted as jungles, seas, deserts, or any alien land. As guardians, they represent the limits of a three-dimensional world. For example, the Khoisan folktales speak of ogres in the dunes, who hunt men. Central African folktales have legends of vertically halved humans who must be negotiated with. Russian peasant lore speak of semi-human Wild Women who live in mountain caves and the Water Grandfather shapeshifter who drowns people in moonlight. The mythic gods of Pan, Sylvanus, and Faunus spark panic in passersby. Policing figures represent the threat against losing conscious awareness over the known world, where the unconscious beckons from the beyond. Only the competent and courageous hero will succeed in penetrating through the barriers.

Again, Campbell resorts to examples of characters who fail this step. In the story of Benares, the hero ventures into a waterless, demon wilderness carting enough water for the trek. But when he finds the guardian ogre, Benares is easily convinced and misled to leave his carts behind as he continues deeper where he was assured more water awaited. The ogre follows, kills, and eats Benares, indicating that not all who risk it have the wherewithal to leave the sanctity of the known world. In Campbell's view, consciousness usurped access to the unconscious.

In the legend of Prince Five Weapons, who was so named for his expertise at wielding so many arms, the prince comes across a sticky-haired ogre who ensnares all the weapons as well as the prince with his gluey tentacles. Before the ogre can eat the prince, however, he convinces the monster that his stomach housed a deadly thunderbolt. Despite losing all his weapons, the prince manages to defeat the ogre by using his wits, proving himself worthy of his role as the Future Buddha. In essence, the hero must abandon the five senses to gain the illusive sixth. Finally, Campbell asserts there's a world-renown motif of polarity, of two clashing rocks that normally crushes the ordinary traveler but through which the hero manages to pass. In this manner, the hero is stripped of his ego before the next step. Thus, only the one truly prepared to sacrifice consciousness shall prove worthy of unconscious rewards.

In the fifth stage, the hero delves into the unconscious by entering the Belly of the Whale, a symbol of the World Womb appearing to take his life before rebirth. Rather than dying therein, the Belly of the Whale is likened to the interior of a temple as a "life-centering, life-renewing act"[5] where the hero's old sense of self dies in a skin-shedding metamorphosis. Dragons, gargoyles, bulls, and demons of all sorts guard the gateway to this pit of despair, another warning against the descent. Those who make it inside are exposed to a heavenly realm.

To establish this proposition, Campbell launches a rapid-fire march of myths from all over the world, without fully threading them to the previous or forthcoming steps. An Eskimo folktale of the hero, Raven, convinces a whale cow to open its mouth in which the hero plunges down into as a bird. The Zulus tell the story of a mother swallowed by an elephant where she finds rivers, forests, and mountains. The Celtic tale of Finn MacCool describes a beast swallowing the hero. Little Red Ridinghood is eaten by a wolf in the German version. In a Polynesian legend, Maui is wholly consumed by his maternal ancestor. The Greek hero Heracles (Roman god, Hercules) dives into the throat of a sea monster to rescue its latest victim. And Kronos devours the entire Greek pantheon, sans Zeus, while in a different space and time, a whale swallows Jonah. Christ is entombed, and Joseph is thrown in a well. Ipso facto, according to Campbell, the Belly of the Whale is a stage in the hero's journey. Whether it belongs at step five in the sequence remains to be seen.

Furthermore, the Twin Heroes of the Navajo acquire the amulets to help them pass the clashing rocks, the cutting reeds, ripping cactuses, and the boiling sands that they cross. In this example, Campbell surreptitiously reverts to the previous step, extolling the dangers of approaching the belly, which for the twins is finding the Sun, who is their father. However, *The Hero with a Thousand Faces* could have benefited from a more extensive examination of the legend in reference to this step. After crossing through the aforementioned four tests, the twins enter the Sun's house, where they meet with the woman of the west cocooned in the four blankets of dawn, daylight, evening, and darkness. When the Sun returns from the day, he hurls his sons against a spiked eastern wall from which they suffer no harm because of the amulet. The Sun puts them in sweltering sauna, which they survive by digging a tunnel. The Sun then invites them to a poisonous smoke from a turquoise pipe off the eastern wall, which the sons inoculate themselves against with the spit of a caterpillar. These are the actual trials of the Twin Heroes in the Belly of the Whale which Campbell could have mentioned to elucidate with greater depth of description what this stage might entail.

Campbell moves on to the model of the sacred king as an analogy for the Belly of the Whale presumably because of the representations of rebirth associated with both. To regenerate a deadened world, the hero sacrifices himself like Christ to restore humanity's favor with God, like Osiris whose flesh is scattered to revitalize the earth, like Attis, the Phrygian god of vegetation, whose self-castration and death restores fecundity to the soil, or like the South Indian King of Quilacare, whose self-mutilation and suicide represented a ritual for a monarchy's renewal and subsequent deification. The king's death is corporeal, while he lives on in the hearts of his subjects by ritual. But it also marks the end of his monomythic journey, calling into question Campbell's use of this as an illustration of this stage. It might have been more appropriate to reference the sacrificed and sacred king in the late stage of Apotheosis, where the hero becomes godlike. The hero of the Belly of the Whale instead, however, emerges onto the Road of Trials, the forthcoming next step, having only experienced a temporary death.

Notably absent from Campbell's examples are the mythic quests into the underworld, the mythic symbol of the World Womb. Persephone is abducted into the underworld where she marries its king, Hades, and becomes Queen of the Underworld. Aeneas brings the Golden Bough to Persephone. Psyche seeks to gain a beauty balm from her. Orpheus tries to rescue his wife from Hades. Dionysus ventures into the underworld to save his mother. Heracles must capture Cerberus, the three-headed dog of the underworld. Theseus attempts to kidnap Persephone on behalf of his brother. The Mongolian King

Gesar descends into the underworld as a part of his initiation as a youth. The Sumerian Queen Inanna descends to visit her twin and Queen of the Underworld, Ereshkigal. Inanna's husband, Dumuzid, and sister-in-law, Geshtinanna, also make the descent. Not attempting to be exhaustive, Campbell leaves the reader to draw their own conclusions on the full experience of the Belly of the Whale with limited examples and circumscribed speculations.

The sixth stage is the Road of Trials in which the hero undergoes a series of ordeals. "There will be a multitude of preliminary victories, unretainable ecstasies, and momentary glimpses of the wonderful land."[6] Campbell stresses that, subject to a dark descent, this is a moment of purification of the soul, where the hero is cleansed for a transcending experience. However, such characterizations are reminiscent of the previous phase. In contrast, all of Campbell's mythological references of this phase involve a series of trials on the way to the underworld, raising the question as to whether this step should have been mentioned before annihilation in the Belly of the Whale. Thus, Campbell refers to the Belly of the Whale as the place where the hero dies in the World Womb, and the Road of Trials as a series of successive tests and a meeting in the underworld, blurring any lines between the two.

Extrapolating from the mythic scenes Campbell sets forth, in essence the hero undergoes a training by tests to determine his capacity and aptitude for self-sacrifice in due course. Psyche must complete four tasks given to her by Aphrodite if she wants to be reunited with Eros. The first three prepare her for the final ordeal of meeting with Persephone. In Inanna's descent, she must pass through seven gates, divesting herself at each turn of an earthly accoutrement, which includes her crown, royal staff, bejeweled necklace, stones of her chest plate, gold ring, the chest plate, and all her garments, in rites of successive passages until she finally arrives naked before the Queen of the Underworld and her twin. Campbell unintentionally blends the previous step with this when he states, "the figure in a myth [. . .] discovers and assimilates his opposite [. . .] either by swallowing it or by being swallowed."[7] Despite having previously covered this and perhaps creating confusion, Campbell indicates that this is another moment where the ego self-annihilates.

Like a shaman, a hero is expected to undertake a journey into the unconscious, whereupon he will encounter symbolic figures as he purifies his soul by cleansing the senses, humbling the self, concentrating wayward energies, and focusing on the transcendent. A Sámi medicine man performs a nightly ceremony in preparation of venturing into the kingdoms of the dead, bringing together tribespeople to witness as he summons spirits. He then undresses to a degree and begins to whirl, calling out, and gesticulating. He beats himself with an axe and grabs burning logs with his hands, until he finally collapses into a trance. Disembodied, his spirit travels to meet with Erlik, Lord of the Underworld, to recover sick souls.

In Campbell's remaining instances of trials, he diverges from mythology to psychotherapy, providing reports of patient dreams and their purported meaning. He employs the same accelerated processional technique. In 1744, Emanuel Swedenborg records a dream about beasts spreading their wings and him flying over them. In 1844, Friedrich Hebbel dreams of being dragged to sea into an abyss. Themistocles dreams of a snake that wrapped around his body and then became an eagle that carried him away. Campbell provides additional dream examples, justifying them as relevant personalized myths. Recall that originally his claim is that all heroic myths of the ancient mythologies of the world may be reduced to a set number of steps. But then at times he relies on reports of individual dreams to establish his point, which is anecdotal and subjective. In this way, Campbell deviates from his original focus on common themes in global myths, weakening the coherence of his argument, shifting ad hoc from a strict hermeneutical approach to a phenomenological one.

At the conclusion of the crisis, the hero comes into the seventh stage with the Meeting with the Goddess. Having successfully overcome the trials, hero is rewarded with a mystical marriage to the Goddess. This stage seems to fit logically after surviving the Belly of the Whale; once the hero comes to the center of the World Womb, he meets the World Creatrix.[8] Mentioned earlier, Brunhild and Sleeping Beauty provided examples of the Refusal of the Call. However, in this stage, Campbell relegates them to a pedestal as paragons of beauty and the "bliss-bestowing goal of every hero's earthly and unearthly quest."[9] Although Campbell initially defines the hero as someone who can be male or female, at this juncture, the hero is decidedly male receiving the reward of a bride. "For she is the incarnation of the promise of perfection; the soul's assurance that, at the conclusion of its exile in a world of organized inadequacies, the bliss that once was known will be known again: the comforting, the nourishing, the 'good' mother—young and beautiful—who was known to us, and even tasted, in the remotest past."[10]

Campbell essentializes women to "mother, sister, mistress, bride."[11] The Goddess is also the Universal Mother, representing the good and the bad in the maternal, "the womb and the tomb."[12] The goddess Diana doesn't take kindly to being spied on in the nude by the Greek hero Actaeon. She wrathfully transforms him into a stag that gets attacked and eaten by his very own hounds. Campbell further plunges his theory into sexism when he proclaims:

Woman, in the picture language of mythology, represents the totality of what can be known. The hero is the one who comes to know. [. . .] [S]he can never be greater than himself, though she can always promise more than he is yet capable of comprehending. She lures, she guides, she bids him burst his fetters [. . .]. Woman is the guide to the sublime acme of sensuous adventure. By deficient eyes she is reduced to inferior states; by the evil eye of ignorance she is spell-bound to banality and ugliness. But she is redeemed by the eyes of understanding. The hero who can take her as she is, without undue commotion but with the kindness and assurance she requires, is potentially the king, the incarnate god, of her created world.[13]

As such the meeting with the goddess is the final test of love for the hero. "The mystical marriage with the queen goddess of the world represents the hero's total mastery of life; for the woman is life, the hero its knower and master."[14]

Belatedly recalling that at times the hero is female, Campbell clarifies that by virtue of her inherent feminine qualities, she is "fit to become the consort of an immortal."[15] Campbell disregards any distaste for coerced relations when he continues, "Then the heavenly husband descends to her and conducts her to his bed—whether she will or no."[16] Despite this stage being about meeting a goddess, female heroes at this juncture instead marry a god, such as the figures of Psyche, the Arapaho girl, the princess of the Frog King, and the Virgin Mary in the Feast of the Assumption, where she ascends to a heavenly bridal chamber.

In the eighth stage, the hero finds the Woman as the Temptress, in which hero has perhaps finally bedded the bride of his dreams, only to discover, like Oedipus, that he has wed his mother, or some such temptress who has sullied his mind, body, or soul. Here Campbell has taken the reader down an unfortunate androcentric—if not misogynistic—corridor, making no allowance for a female hero's encounter of this stage except as a passive beneficiary. Further, this raises the question as to the necessity of this separate step if it's simply another encounter with the goddess, which has already been duly canvassed by the Meeting with the Goddess.

Campbell relays the lesson of Saint Peter whose daughter was so beautiful, he prayed for her sickness to avoid inciting temptation in others. She fell ill until she found God, and Saint Peter restored her health through prayer. But when a pagan king wanted to marry her, she embarked on a hunger strike until she died—the virgin martyr too beautiful for her own good. This same story could have been told from a different perspective. Perhaps she was too beautiful and burdened by unwanted advances. Rather than marry, she chose a monastic life—a spiritual marriage to God. Subjected to slanderous claims by rejected suitors, she stays true to her convictions for which she is eventually martyred and elevated to the status of Saint by those who venerated her. Viewed from this angle, she's a goddess not unlike Psyche, and her story belongs in the discussion of the previous stage.

In general, Campbell describes this as an instance in the restriction of a hero's consciousness, where one is farthest from relating to the unconscious and benefiting from its mysteries, where one is caught up in the profanest of moments rather than at ease in a spiritual world. "[W]hen it suddenly dawns on us [. . .] that everything we think [. . .] is necessarily tainted with the odor of the flesh, then [. . .] there is experienced a moment of revulsion: life, the acts of life, the organs of life, woman in particular as the great symbol of life, become intolerable to the pure, the pure, pure soul."[17] As a result, women become a symbol of defeat.[18] Campbell links women with the primeval enemy of men, citing examples of monks devoted to worship yet tempted by women. He continues to the end of the chapter with a discussion of temptations by the devil as a metonym for women.

The next stage of the journey is an Atonement with the Father, an atonement giving rise to an "at-one-ment" in which the hero releases the dual fears of God and sin. These fears are projected upon a dangerous father or wrathful God. Overcoming these fears requires an ego abandonment with the help of the ego-shatterer—the father. For the male hero, the father symbolizes a future task, and for a female hero, according to Campbell, the father represents a future husband. By way of explaining, Campbell further digresses into another gendered, essentializing dichotomy between sons and daughters, the former who master the universe and the latter to become the mastered universe. Yet, there appears to be no real impediment for simply allowing the possibility that the father could represent the challenge of a future for both sons and daughters in their respective universes to master. The narrow interpretation of mythology to restrict the domain of women to domestic avenues limits the applicability of the monomyth to men. If only men can be masters of the universe, then how can women also be its heroes?

In this step, the father can be terrifying, and the hero may find hope and support in the masculine's reflection, a feminine figure. For instance, the Navajo Twin Warriors gain support from the Spider Woman to find their father, Sun, who puts them through a series of trials before he accepts them. Campbell argues that only the truly tested can be admitted into the father's house. Otherwise, they will suffer the fate of Phaethon, who wished to wield the sun's power by commanding his father's chariot for a day. Unable to follow his father's path, Phaethon runs wild, firing the heavens and scorching the earth until Zeus shoots him with a thunderbolt, plunging him to his death in the blaze of a falling star. Phaethon demonstrates the cautionary tale of the poorly initiated, the improperly prepared by the mystagogue. Alternatively, however, Phaethon, son of a water nymph and a solar deity, can also be viewed as a monitory myth against following too closely in the steps of the paternal. From the outset, Phaethon had no hope of controlling the chariot because it was calibrated for the weight of his father. Plato describes the soul as being made up of the charioteer and two horses, one wild and one tamed. From this perspective, charioting a father's soul leads to madness—not atonement.

In Indigenous Australian mythologies, the Great Father Snake initiates the son in a series of rituals releasing his "hero-penis"[19] from its foreskin, marking the transition from an attachment to the breast to a discovery of the power of the phallus. For Campbell, these rites dramatize the Oedipal complex, sublimating the patricidal impulse and symbolically satisfying a sanguinary thirst that culminates in a circumcision in lieu of castration. Here Campbell reveals an ethnocentric bias by applying a colonizing filter:

> There can be no doubt that no matter how unilluminated the stark-naked Australian savages may seem to us, their symbolical ceremonials represent a survival into modern times of an incredibly old system of spiritual instruction, the far-flung evidences of which are to be found not only in all the lands and islands bordering the Indian Ocean, but also among the remains of the archaic centers of what we tend to regard as our own very special brand of civilization.[20]

Nonetheless, Campbell emphasizes that their lore retains value for all.

In pursuit of patriarchal power, mythologies of filicide represent sacrifice, resurrection, and renewal as in the cases of Dionysus, Tammuz, Adonis, Mithra, Virbius, Attis, Ottis, and Jesus Christ. The contradictory father represents the giver and taker of life, "the fountainhead of all opposites."[21] Campbell strings together disparate examples of the all-powerful and the powerless, such as the mighty figure of Viracocha wandering as a mendicant, Mary and Joseph begging for shelter, Zeus and Hermes asking for hospitality, Edshu disseminating chaos as a form of pleasure, and Allah, responding to all prayers from a supplicant anywhere as the All-Present, All-Powerful. The author concludes by stating that the father represents the paradox of creation, a "germinal secret" that "can never be quite explained."[22] Using another gendered argument, Campbell sweepingly claims that "in every system of theology there is an umbilical point, an Achilles tendon which the finger of the mother- life has touched, and where the possibility of perfect knowledge has been impaired."[23] Thus a theology streaming with imperfect knowledge results from the profanity of being born to a woman. Once the hero exposes himself to the horrors of the profane world to conquer and eliminate all vestiges of the maternal, then only can he glimpse the sacred and truly atone. In this way, Campbell indirectly blames women for holding men back by their umbilical cords, which must be severed to attain heavenly insights. Campbell concludes with a comparison to Job, who in the Biblical tradition atoned to God for despair. Having argued for atonement from an entirely male perspective, that a man is destined to liberate his champion phallus and master the world, Campbell doesn't realize that he's written women out of the journey. The universal journey he argues that belongs to every man and woman is essentially a male journey, or one that preemptively ends for women in the silence of Freudian phallic wishes.

Upon atoning, the hero transcends earthly life and enters into a divine state, in Apotheosis, the tenth step of the monomyth, because he has annihilated his consciousness and freed himself of fear. The hero has become as godlike as Buddha and has assumed his full potential where pain or pleasure have no command. Again, by Campbell's definition, a woman might not reach this stage in the absence of an atonement that she's been excluded from. The hero, however, surpasses gender norms in apotheosis, becoming man and woman because as a divinity, he transmutes opposites into androgyny. Examples of he-she gods and the godlike include Avalokiteshvara, Awonawilona, Ardhanarisha, Tiresias, Adam before Eve, Hermaphrodite, Psyche's child, and the God of Genesis. But for the hero, these examples do not present references for becoming godlike, which should have been Campbell's focus. The existence of androgynous figures in mythology does not mean that being born a god is the equivalent of striving to attain godhood.

For Campbell, in accordance with certain Abrahamic traditions, cosmogony begins with Adam's rib, the removal of the feminine into a separate form, which results in the fall of man, the discovery of opposites, and the introduction of time. At the end of the cosmogenic cycle, the hero restores both halves as he returns to heaven, which in this iteration doesn't appear to include women. In ritual, Campbell claims that traditional Aboriginal and Torres Strait Islander people undergo a follow-up initiation into manhood a year after circumcision to create a subincision, which results in a "penis womb," symbolic of the male vagina.[24] Notwithstanding Campbell's allusion to a male preoccupation with womb-envy, a hero's apotheosis reflects a balance between the feminine and masculine natures. To explain this, however, Campbell continues with binary contrasts, where one subsumes the other.

The hero confronts trials in an effort to initiate him into becoming a man and realizing that he was the father all along. "We in Him, and He in us," Campbell contends, and by theocentric implication, He is also God.[25] In this account, men have a more specialized relationship with God. Campbell argues that while male and female are two halves of a whole, men are the antecedents (an assumption that is challenged by second wave feminism and Simone de Beauvoir in *The Second Sex* which was incidentally published in the same year as *The Hero with a Thousand Faces*).[26] The path of the hero is reflected in the three wonders of the myth of the Bodhisattva, where the first wonder exposes the bisexual nature of man. The second wonder is the discovery of the inner world of eternity with an egoless center—the attainment of Nirvana. The third wonder is that time and eternity are symbolized by the hermaphroditic form, where the world of time represents the mother's womb of darkness and eternity represents the light of the father.

Campbell concludes this chapter with the Tibetan perspective of the union between Buddhas and Bodhisattvas, in which one sex is not preferenced over the other. All things in apotheosis are simultaneously worldly and ethereal, temporal and eternal, profane and sacred—at once created in the image of a he-she god. In this way, the hero attains enlightenment. In the Tibetan view, the state of Nirvana is available to both men and women. But Campbell misses an opportunity to enrich this chapter with a discussion on the gnostic experiences of the divine from Jewish tzadiks, Christian saints, Muslim walis, Hindu rishis, Sikh gurus, and Shintoist kannushi.

Receiving the Ultimate Boon is step eleven of the monomyth, where hero learns that he is a king among men, indestructible under the vicissitudes of life and impervious to loss. His soul cannot be touched, almost as if it were removed to another plane of existence with eternal sustenance and healing. The hero discovers heaven on earth, hugged the Cosmic Bear, suckles milk from Heidrun, eats the manna, drinks from the Tree of Life, imbibes the fermented juice of the gods, and laps from the rivers of paradise. He returns to the source, recalling something previously known to him, reality before consciousness, the place beyond thinking, feeling, or symbols. Like Dante, the monomythic hero ventures past the unknown and bathed in the eternal light. As part of his indestructible body, he can exist outside of a corporeal form, leave his body and yet still remain a part of it.

The miraculous, immortalizing energy is often guarded by gods, and the hero might have to embark on a final quest to seize their treasure. Here Campbell cites the Sumerian Epic of Gilgamesh, where Gilgamesh travels across the waters of death to the Everlasting Island and meets with the Flood King, the archetypal father, who instructs him on how to find the plant of eternal life at the bottom of the sea. Gilgamesh proceeds to capture the seaweed at great risk and physical cost and returns to the land. Thus, the hero attains the power of youth. Yet, Gilgamesh loses the kelp when a snake steals it from him, giving the snake the power to shed its skin and be reborn, to the utter dismay of Gilgamesh. While this hero seemingly captures the Ultimate Boon, Campbell hardly explains its sudden loss. In fact, Gilgamesh subsequently becomes King of the Underworld in a later version of the myth. Instead of an example where the hero loses the boon, Campbell could have used the examples of the Greek myth of Jason's quest for the Golden Fleece, the fairy tale of the Golden Goose, the Persian epic of Khidr in search of the fountain of youth, or the Sufi poem, *The Conference of the Birds*, where the hoopoe leads the fowl congress to the abode of enlightenment.

Not without a negative example, Campbell references the myth of King Midas, who is gifted with the golden touch and accidentally transforms his beloved daughter into a gilded statue. For Campbell, the Ultimate Boon devolves to the capacities and limitation of the recipient. Instead of obtaining the true boon, the hero settles for longer life, additional resources for his people, or the removal of hardships. In consequence, where the hero might have earned greater insight, he settles for immediacy. This then appears to negate the hero's mission, and the monomyth presents a conundrum. If the hero truly annihilated his ego, then he would never settle for anything egotistical. A lesser hero, perhaps—one who only successfully conquered a portion of self-interest or certain fears. Under such conditions, however, can it be said that the hero has attained enlightenment? Has he truly become worthy of the Ultimate Boon?

In the twelfth step, the hero experiences a Refusal of Return. Having found immortality, there's a reluctance to return to the world of old. Nonetheless, his quest demands that he share the boon with others, to heal and renew the land. But the hero often gets caught up in the ecstasy of the eternal, and he may delay homecoming because for now, in fact, he's discovered his true home. He's loath to leave it. In the Refusal of the Return, Campbell offers the exemplar of King Muchukunda, a man born of a motherless miracle out of his father's left side. He is a king among kings and ascended to the heavens to champion the gods in their centurieslong battle against the demons. In return, they gift him with a boon of his desire. He requests uninterrupted sleep for the rest of his days to be woken on pain of death by fire.

The King sleeps for centuries but awakens one day when he's was mistaken for an enemy by a warrior king who battled with Lord Krishna. The warrior king is instantly smote with fire by King Muchukunda. When the smoke cleared, Lord Krishna appears before him, much to Muchukunda's relief. When he steps out of the cave, Muchukunda finds that in the centuries that passed, people and things have shrunk. He's too large for the world and retreats further up the mountain, never to be seen again. Campbell concludes that this is an example of someone who refused to return with the treasure.

However, Campbell conveniently leaves out salient details of this myth. Muchukunda fought with the gods for hundreds of years. When the battle was over, he returned to his people, but everyone he knew had passed on; all of his possessions were gone. There was no one to share his successes with. In view of this, he asks for eternal, undisturbed rest, which is granted. According to some other versions of this myth, Muchukunda does not receive *moksha*, salvation, the Ultimate Boon. When Lord Krishna materializes at the end, Muchukunda takes refuge in his lord, humbly submitting that he'd been wrongly caught up in world deeds. Krishna promises moksha, as the prize for best karma that can only be attained through penance, which Muchukunda submits to in his retreat up the mountain. Thus, it's arguable whether Muchukunda received an Ultimate Boon from the gods as a reward for his service, but if he did, it's also apparent that he had returned to his people. In effect, the moral appears to be that if a hero chases worldly glory he risks losing his world. Without additional examples, Campbell makes thin work of establishing this moment as a legitimate step a hero takes on his monomythic quest. Rather, the myth of King Muchukunda would have served better as an example of the previous step, the Ultimate Boon. Other possible examples reflective of a so-called Refusal of Return could have included the story of Odysseus who spends years traveling before actually returning home after the Trojan War. When he finally reaches Ithaca, he is hesitant to reveal his true identity and take up his role as king, preferring instead to continue wandering.

In addition, in some versions of the Arthurian legend, King Arthur is mortally wounded in battle and taken to the isle of Avalon to be healed. He is said to still be alive, waiting to return when Britain needs him most. Or possibly the biblical account of Moses, who guides the Israelites out of slavery in Egypt and receives the Ten Commandments from God. However, when he returns to the people, he discovers them worshipping a golden calf and is hesitant to continue leading them. Or, also Siddhartha Gautama, who achieves enlightenment and becomes the Buddha. He is reluctant to teach others, as he believes that the truths he has discovered cannot be fully expressed in words. Finally, a mythopoeic example is Frodo Baggins from *The Lord of the Rings*, who sets out on a quest to destroy the One Ring and save Middle-Earth. When it's done, he is reluctant to return home to the Shire, as he has been forever changed by his experiences.

When the hero does return to his people, he experiences a Magic Flight, aided by the supernatural, as the thirteenth step. To explain this, Campbell refers to the Welsh hero Gwion Bach who journeys to the bottom of a lake and meets with the magician Caridwen. She instructs him to stir her cauldron for a year in order to receive three drops of inspiration. However, the pot spews drops onto Gwion which makes him realize that his quest was to avoid Caridwen, a formidable sorceress. In fear, he flees. A mad chase ensues. With his newfound power, he changes into a hare to run faster. She changes into its predator. He changes into a fish and jumps in a river. She follows as an otter. He flies out in the shape of a bird. She morphs into a hawk. He sees a wheat pile and shrinks into a grain. She transforms into a hen and swallows the grain, carrying him for nine months. At that point, she's no longer interested in vengeance. Instead, she casts him off to sea. Clearly, this is a case of magical flight, but is it an example of a monomythic stage? The hero's quest was to avoid the witch, instead he fails and she consumes him. This seems to indicate that running from a powerful force may not be the right course and allowing it to pass through the hero or the hero through it is the lesson. This hero fought to escape the call of the feminine, but in the end incorporating her energy made him born again, beautiful and unblemished.

Campbell gives another negative lesson, magical flight gone wrong, in the Siberian myth of Morgon-Kara, who was such a powerful shaman, he could bring back the dead. To test this claim, the High God traps a man's soul in a bottle under his thumb. Morgon-Kara discovers the secret, transforms himself into a wasp, stings the High God, and restores the dead man to life. This angers the High God, and as retribution he diminishes the shaman's power. Here Campbell negates his point about magical flight. It might not be such a good thing.

Magical flight might occur in the form of obstacles set forth before the hero's opponent, "magical obstruction and evasion," hindering the antagonist with successive impediments of charmed objects that allows the hero time to escape.[27] This can be seen in a Māori myth of the woman who swallows her two sons, the Grimm fairy tale of The Water Nixie, the Japanese legendary descent and return of Izanagi, and the Greek hero, Jason, who flees the king by slaying the king's son and casting the body to sea in small parts, which causes the king to pursue the body parts and not Jason. Campbell concludes with a short mention of the Greek myth Orpheus and Eurydice, arguing that the obstacle to this magical flight was human frailty. However, Orpheus is another example of a hero who did not, in fact, fulfill his quest of bringing back his wife from the underworld without gazing upon her.

The hero may have difficulty returning because the bliss of the boon attained is so awe-inspiring he is stunned into a paralysis that requires a Rescue from Without in step fourteen. A deep sleep may befall him or he may be in a sense dead to the world, and like Sleeping Beauty, in need of an external force to shake the slumber off. Referring back to the Eskimo hero who became a raven to plunge into the belly of the whale, Raven becomes trapped in a dying giant that eventually washes ashore. Other people discover the carcass and cut into it, releasing the raven hero.

Campbell also references the sun-goddess of Japan, Amaterasu, whose storm-god brother frightens her into a cave for concealment, except that this has the unintended of consequence of destroying the earth. Eight million gods assemble in dance and offering, which piques Amaterasu's curiosity enough to step outside once again, in effect rescuing her from a paralytic fear. Little Red Ridinghood whose eaten by a wolf, escapes its belly only when a hunter shoots him. Inanna, who visits her sister and Queen of the Underworld, is flayed and hung for dead by Ereshkigal. When Inanna doesn't return to earth, her servant appeals to the air god who sends creatures of food and of water to enliven her. Ultimately, this stage reflects the impact of contact with the unconscious. Though it may arrest the hero, the unconscious will aid in his resurrection.

At last, the hero Crosses the Return Threshold, in step fifteen. The hero must maintain cognizance of the fact that the divine and human realms are simply two aspects of one world. The hero explores the heavenly dimension to enrich the earthly one. Campbell references the Dutch Catskill mountains legend of Rip van Winkle, a duty shirker who escapes the call of responsibility, as embodied by a termagant spouse, into the mountains where he falls asleep for so long that, when he returns, the country has transformed into an independent nation. Rip doesn't return with a boon but does return to an idle life now free of the nagging wife, providing another sample of Campbell's heroic missteps. In fact, the world seems to improve in van Winkle's absence.

Campbell then refers to the Irish legend of Oisin, son of Finn MacCool, who marries a fairy and becomes king of the Otherworld. After three hundred years, Oisin wishes to visit Ireland again, but the fairy warns against this, giving him a white steed who will protect him from having to step into his old world. If he does, he will instantly become an old blind man, forever severed from the Otherworld. Thus, Oisin reenters his father's kingdom, but unfortunately falls off his horse, fulfilling the dark prophecy and failing his quest as hero to thread together the two dimensions of the one world. However, Campbell uses Oisin's horse as an example of the requirements of protecting one's sanctity from the impurity of the profane world, just as the Emperor Montezuma never sets foot on the ground, the king of Persia only walks new carpets, and the royalty of Uganda do not touch the earth because the sacred man may lose the charge of his divine trust if it's drained by direct contact with dirt. To this end, Campbell views certain modern conduct as reflective of this sacred embodiment, such as when the Englishman finds it necessary to wear a dinner coat in the Nigerian jungles, a nun adopts medieval costume, or the original tradition of encircling a wife's finger with a ring—to insulate the sacred against the profane. Unfortunately, Campbell's examples are also nativistic, patronizing, and biased. The Englishman's dinner coat is a colonizing symbol of superiority, an analogy that also confers a white savior complex upon the hero. Circumscribing a woman's dress, whether as a bride of God or man, also reinforces the power structure of patriarchy. But the critical takeaway idea here is that in returning home, there should be some symbol of preservation for the sacred status achieved or knowledge gained when Crossing the Return Threshold.

Campbell concludes with a final successful illustration of Kamar al-Zaman who meets Princess Badur in his sleep by an arrangement of a couple of wily jinns. The young royals both instantly fall in love and exchange rings. When they awake, Kamar al-Zaman is desolate to find that Princess Badur is not with him. So begins the journey of bringing their two worlds together. While this appears to be a crossing of the threshold, it's not a crossing of the return threshold that Campbell alludes to. Instead, the return occurs when they reunite again and Kamar brings the Princess back to his kingdom.

The hero at last becomes Master of the Two Worlds in step sixteen. He has humbly stood before God and glimpsed the universe in its entirety. In doing so, hero has transcended his fears, desires, ambitions, hopes, limitations, and his ego to behold the truth and retain its bliss. His capacity to know ultimate truth and simultaneously exist on an earthly plain gives him a certain unique comprehension of life. According to Campbell, he's represented in mythology by figures such as the drifting beggar, the migrant musician, and the gods Odin, Viracocha, and Edshu. To others, he may be reviled or respected, appearing as a fool, sage, nomad, or a familiar stranger.

Campbell concludes the monomyth with the Freedom to Live as the seventeenth step. Having witnessed the reality of the cosmos and understood his place in it, the hero can at last fully experience life without becoming attached to it. Attachments and resistance to change cause the frictions that lead to the journey. Nature inevitably renews the world, but nothing perishes. The hero returns to a state of primordial innocence with the manifested consciousness of truth, as exemplified by Jesus who spoke as a newborn.[28] Campbell reverts back to Gwion Bach who was swallowed by Caridwen for nine months whereupon she gave birth to him as a baby who proceeds to speak truth to power. In conclusion, the freedom to live is evidenced in the fairy tale of Little Briar Rose, a version of Sleeping Beauty where the Prince of Eternity kisses the Princess of the World. Not only does Little Briar Rose awaken, but so does everyone and everything around her. Without conscious realization of the unconscious, people are in essence sleepwalking. When the unconscious comes knocking, and the hero awakens to reality, then only will the hero truly be alive.

In seventeen steps, Campbell sets forth the universal journey purportedly traveled by all heroes. His claim is supported by a limited number of disconnected examples that are at times repetitive, confusing, insufficient, misappropriated, and altogether antithetical to his point. In addition, his arguments in places have been stridently nativistic, antireligion, and privileged, making it difficult on the reader to parse through for underlying significance. On the completion of his discussion, he claims that the steps are so simple that they "defy description," which was actually what he accomplished. He defied describing what he set out to do. He also argues that not all of the steps are strictly necessary to the quest. Some may be skipped; others may be repeated. Campbell's conclusion is that there is a journey, but it's not so universally consistent as originally thought. He then proceeds to decry all the damage that's been done to myth through obscuration, implying that it caused the inconsistency. Oral storytelling is not a reliable form of transmission. Successive generations transmute and retool symbols for current purpose, rendering them, at times, nonsensical. Concurrently, this is what he encourages moderns to do with scripture. Whether or not Jesus actually existed shouldn't matter. The real importance is the symbol of his existence, obfuscating religious "myths" in the same way he impugns others for confounding ancient myths.

Notwithstanding the deficiencies in his argument, the question of a universal mythic quest remains, particularly in the light of mythopoetic works of C. S. Lewis, J. R. R. Tolkien, and George Lucas. Campbell wasn't the first person to posit the existence of structure from myth. Writers have been lifting it, consciously or subconsciously, for centuries. To fill the lacuna left by Campbell, it behooves us first to examine the psychological justifications for the monomyth. After that, I will demonstrate how the monomyth can be rescued from its befuddled proofs by reassembling the steps in an order that more appropriately reflects psychological development of growth into adulthood and subsequent maturation. In this respect, rather than using disconnected, unrelated examples, I demonstrate that every step of the monomyth can be contained in a single story.

NOTES

1. Campbell, *Hero*, 58.

2. Campbell, *The Hero with a Thousand Faces*, 48. All quotes from Joseph Campbell's *The Hero with a Thousand Faces* Copyright © Joseph Campbell Foundation (jcf.org) 2008. Used with permission.

3. Campbell, *The Hero with a Thousand Faces*, 48. All quotes from Joseph Campbell's *The Hero with a Thousand Faces* Copyright © Joseph Campbell Foundation (jcf.org) 2008. Used with permission.

4. Campbell, *The Hero with a Thousand Faces*, 53–54. All quotes from Joseph Campbell's *The Hero with a Thousand Faces* Copyright © Joseph Campbell Foundation (jcf.org) 2008. Used with permission.

5. Campbell, *Hero*, 92.

6. Campbell, *The Hero with a Thousand Faces*, 90. All quotes from Joseph Campbell's *The Hero with a Thousand Faces* Copyright © Joseph Campbell Foundation (jcf.org) 2008. Used with permission.

7. Campbell, *The Hero with a Thousand Faces*, 89. All quotes from Joseph Campbell's *The Hero with a Thousand Faces* Copyright © Joseph Campbell Foundation (jcf.org) 2008. Used with permission.

8. Campbell, *Hero*, 114.

9. Campbell, *Hero*, 110–11.

10. Campbell, *The Hero with a Thousand Faces*, 92. All quotes from Joseph Campbell's *The Hero with a Thousand Faces* Copyright © Joseph Campbell Foundation (jcf.org) 2008. Used with permission.

11. Campbell, *Hero*.

12. Campbell, *Hero*, 114.

13. Campbell, *The Hero with a Thousand Faces*, 97. All quotes from Joseph Campbell's *The Hero with a Thousand Faces* Copyright © Joseph Campbell Foundation (jcf.org) 2008. Used with permission.

14. Campbell, *The Hero with a Thousand Faces*, 101. All quotes from Joseph Campbell's *The Hero with a Thousand Faces* Copyright © Joseph Campbell Foundation (jcf.org) 2008. Used with permission.

15. Campbell, *Hero*, 119.

16. Campbell, *The Hero with a Thousand Faces*, 99. All quotes from Joseph Campbell's *The Hero with a Thousand Faces* Copyright © Joseph Campbell Foundation (jcf.org) 2008. Used with permission.

17. Campbell, *The Hero with a Thousand Faces*, 102. All quotes from Joseph Campbell's *The Hero with a Thousand Faces* Copyright © Joseph Campbell Foundation (jcf.org) 2008. Used with permission.

18. Campbell, *Hero*, 123.

19. Campbell, *Hero*, 138.

20. Campbell, *The Hero with a Thousand Faces*, 119. All quotes from Joseph Campbell's *The Hero with a Thousand Faces* Copyright © Joseph Campbell Foundation (jcf.org) 2008. Used with permission. In addition, the universal applicability of the Oedipal Complex to the global south has been challenged by its members. See Frantz Fanon, *Black Skin, White Masks* (New York: Grove Press, 1967).

21. Campbell, *Hero*, 145.

22. Campbell, *Hero*, 147.

23. Campbell, *The Hero with a Thousand Faces*, 124. All quotes from Joseph Campbell's *The Hero with a Thousand Faces* Copyright © Joseph Campbell Foundation (jcf.org) 2008. Used with permission.

24. Campbell, *Hero*, 154.

25. Campbell, *Hero*, 161.

26. Simone de Beauvoir, *The Second Sex*, trans. H. M. Parshley (New York: Alfred A. Knopf, 1993).

27. Campbell, *Hero*, 197.

28. See J. K. Elliott and M. R. James, *The Apocryphal New Testament: A Collection of Apocryphal Christian Literature in an English Translation* (Oxford: Oxford University Press, 1993); Seyyed Hossein Nasr, *The Study Quran: A New Translation and Commentary* (New York: HarperOne, 2015), 19:29–34.

Chapter 3

On Jungian Psychology

A Primer on Individuation

Like his predecessors, Joseph Campbell utilizes principles of psychoanalysis as a theoretical framework for the hero's journey. As a mid-twentieth-century publication, *The Hero with a Thousand Faces* relies upon Freudian and Jungian psychology, but Campbell's description of the hero is more Jungian.[1] For Carl Jung, "myths are first and foremost psychic phenomena that reveal the nature of the soul."[2] Because post-Campbellian theorists Christopher Vogler and Maureen Murdock continue use of the same conceptual framework (albeit from a post-Jungian perspective) and their works are further delved into in Chapters Four and Five, this study focuses on Jungian and post-Jungian theories as it relates to character development in the hero and heroine's journey.

The term psychology originally derives from the Greek word "psyche," which means soul. Psychology then is a kind of science of the soul. The question then arises: what is the process by which a person may understand their psyche; know their own soul? Jung calls this a process of individuation, a term he coined to describe the path of "coming to selfhood" or "self-realization."[3] He contends that the psyche constitutes a composite of consciousness and the unconscious, wherein the Ego personifies the master of consciousness while the Self represents the seat of the unconscious and is structured by that inherent polarity. Post-Jungian psychologists understand that the foundation of a psyche's vitality derives from that polar tension, when one polarity is stressed, the energy of the other will pull it to the opposite. The main polarities of the psyche for this discussion are Ego and Self, consciousness and the unconscious, masculine and feminine. Recall that Alfred Adler viewed polarities as a kind of neurosis necessitating psychotherapy. Despite a seeming binarism the two opposites are not mutually exclusive. Both exist as a contiguous, compensating, replenishing pairing of a whole system.

Consciousness represents all that one may become aware of about the world and who we are as individuals within it. The unconscious represents the vast unknown—be it of the mind or of the unseen. For Jung, this includes the personal unconscious which constitute processes of the mind that one is unaware of such as repressed feelings, instinctual perception, automatic reactions, subconscious behavior, and complexes. It also includes the collective unconscious, a deeper level of the unconscious shared with all of humanity by heredity that contain archetypal energies.

Consciousness and the unconscious are not mutually exclusive experiences of the psyche. Rather, consciousness emerges from the unconscious, being that subset of information that we become aware of. At birth, the undifferentiated Self exists in a primordial muddle with the Ego where it completely identifies with the Self in an expanded state. The Ego is the Self and Self is the Ego; and there is limited, if any, conscious awareness. In this moment, there is a sense of wholeness and perfection—the Self deified.

Because of a preponderance of feminine energy to which an Ego is born (of woman, from womb), the polarizing force of the masculine principle of the psyche triggers consciousness development by pulling the Ego away from the Self. Jung refers to the attraction of opposite psychological functions as *enantiodromia,* which he defines as "the emergence of the unconscious opposite in the course of time. This characteristic phenomenon practically always occurs when an extreme, one-sided tendency dominates conscious life; in time an equally powerful counter position is built up, which first inhibits the conscious performance and subsequently breaks through the conscious control."[4] There's an eager and natural instinct to develop one's Ego as separate and distinct from its source, embarking on a journey of discovery. The Ego learns through projection and differentiation. In doing so, a person may experience over-identification with a parent, a role, a flaw, or a desire and alternatively feel alienated. The challenge for the Ego is to understand its identity and limitations apart from others—it is to individuate. Jung labels this a process of individuation, the continuing object of which is to increase consciousness.

Once the Ego has been alienated from the Self, the Ego can begin to encounter the Self as something separate from itself and heed the Self's call for reintegration. In other words, having spent so much time being driven by a preponderance of masculine energies to individuate, a polar imbalance results and the feminine principle of the psyche pulls the Ego back to reunite with the Self.[5] Consequently, the Ego and Self undergo a process to become whole again with self-knowledge compelled by an innate impulse to consciously realize itself—Self-realization. Ultimately, individuation results in a condition in which the Ego relates to the Self without being characterized by it. When the Ego properly reintegrates into the Self without being subsumed or lost within it, then consciousness and the unconscious can exchange information seamlessly.

Accordingly, the process of individuation may be divided into two phases: the first half of life and the second—the first half being marked by de-integration from the Self and the second half with reintegration. Jungian psychologist Edward F. Edinger argues that "[t]he current working formula [. . .] is, first half of life: ego-Self separation; second half of life: ego-Self reunion."[6] Swiss post-Jungian psychologist Jolande Jacobi further expounds upon the two phases in the context of enantiodromia:

> It is implied from the very beginning in Jung's work that psychological growth in the second half of life must be preceded by another which alone will enable man to face the tremendous demands he will meet at that stage. [. . .] Development in the first half of life has its own form and its own laws which could be described as an "initiation into adulthood." When completed it represents the first stage on the way of individuation. [. . .] A certain one-sidedness is both important and necessary in this first phase of life, since only thus can one be capable of the unreflecting activity that is requisite to the conquest of a place in the world. This has the disadvantage of unconsciousness but the advantage of an inexhaustible capacity for fighting one's way through in the struggle of existence.[7]

In other words, the Ego's initial journey to individuate may be viewed as part of the process of a person's coming-of-age experience, while the Ego's return to the Self a part of coming of middle age. "It is a question of moving from an 'ego-centered' attitude to an 'ego-transcending' one [. . .]."[8]

Both phases of individuation occur through interactions with symbols which represent the language of the unconscious, containing psychic energy that are not consciously known but nonetheless provide information that the mind perceives. Jung believed that "Only the symbolic life can express the need of the soul [. . .]."[9] As the term implies, symbols are images with patent import but also latent. Symbols can be used consciously with words or produced unconsciously in dreams, serving to crystallize the experience of transformation during individuation.

Reintegrating with the unconscious requires a set of symbols strung together to reflect a form of an ideal—an archetype—at once an innate behavior and a primary image or emotion. Drawing on Plato's Theory of Forms in which Plato postulated a higher, nontangible essence to all things, Jung coined the term "archetype" to define analogous perceptions of the psyche that are primordial, universal, and unconscious. Archetypes allow the "psychic phenomena" found in the unconscious to become conscious and may appear as symbols or a patterned behavior. Archetypes may be of situation (such as a quest), character (such as a mentor), or opposites (such as good versus evil, old versus young, masculine versus feminine) and may constitute a psychological analogue to biological instinct. In distinguishing between symbol and archetype, the Self, for instance, represents an archetype of psychic wholeness, which is symbolized by mandalas and various images of roundness. For Jung, archetypes arise from the well of the collective unconscious that human beings dip into to restore balance between an exaggerated Ego and an unknown Self. Critics have found this claim to be far-reaching, debating the provability of an inherited, shared collective unconscious. Jung also noted parallels between his conception of archetypes and those to be found in mythological motifs, but for Jung, they exist primordially in the mind.[10] Here queer theorists take issue with some of the essentializing aspects of his theory where he relates gender or sex to immutable aspects of the mind. Post-Jungian psychologists, however, have stepped away from Jung's universalisms. Regardless of whether archetypes are universal or primordial, human beings find and utilize archetypes elsewhere, such as in myth, history, religion, philosophy, art, and literature.

The Ego's initial archetypal guides in individuation are the polar duo of the Persona and the Shadow. The Persona archetype represents the mask a person wears in adopting social roles or functions, allowing the Ego to mediate between itself and people. For example, society often dictates what it means to be a good son or daughter. Adopting that function serves the Ego's development, becoming that function to the exclusion of all other personality attributes creates imbalance in the psyche and gives rise to its polar opposite, the Shadow. Engagement with the Persona allows a person to become strong in one's identity in society without becoming that identity. The more one over-identifies, however, with the Persona archetype, the darker the Shadow archetype becomes.

The Shadow represents the dark elements of the personality that have been repressed for the sake of an ideal Persona—those parts of the Ego that have been judged weak and wanting. Instead of incorporating parts of the Ego that a person might fear in themselves, they make the mistake of repressing it. In some respects, the stronger its repression, the more powerful the Shadow archetype becomes. Employing the myth of the hero battling the dragon, Jung asserts that the hero "must realize that the shadow exists and that he can draw strength from it [. . .] i.e., before the ego can triumph, it must master and assimilate the shadow."[11] The Shadow warehouses everything that shames or embarrasses a person such as laziness, anger, cowardice, lying, obsession, selfishness, greed, or other unacceptable desires. Jung further describes the Shadow as:

> a moral problem that challenges the whole ego-personality, for no one can become conscious of the shadow without considerable moral effort. To become

conscious of it involves recognizing the dark aspects of the personality as present and real. This act is the essential condition for any kind of self-knowledge, and it therefore, as a rule, meets with considerable resistance. Indeed, self-knowledge as a psychotherapeutic measure frequently requires much painstaking work extending over a period of time.[12]

Another significant polar coupling to serve as archetypal guides into the unconscious are the sexual and contrasexual other. Jung describes the archetypal masculine and feminine aspects of the psyche as Anima and Animus, respectively, but the post-Jungian theorists developed it more fully. The Anima represents the archetype symbolizing the feminine energy in a person's psyche, while the Animus symbolizes the masculine energy of a person's psyche. Jung refers to them as the "foundation stones of the psychic structure," forming a "divine pair."[13] Encountering and incorporating a psyche's sexual and contrasexual archetypes fosters reintegration with the Self.

Jungian psychologist Edward Whitmont takes this further by drawing on Chinese tradition and comparing Anima and Animus to Yin and Yang, where the Yin is yonic, encompassing, receptive, lunar, of the earth and of the soul while Yang is phallic, creative, powerful, solar, of the heavens and of the spirit.[14] The challenge for the Ego is to bring balance to these opposing internal forces, which begins with an imbalance, being entirely contained by the Self at birth and born of feminine energies. As such, at birth the Ego is completely subsumed by the Anima. The countervailing attraction of the masculine principle draws the Ego out, by force of polarity, into social orientation, unrelentingly demanding its due expression until the Ego is fully realized. Those who are born predisposed to act on Animus energy may find it easier than those subsumed by the Anima principle. Once the Ego fully develops its identity, as aided by the Animus, it feels an overwhelming draw back to the Anima, through enantiodromia, thereby ushering in the return to the Self. Those with a cognitive preference for the Anima as may have developed through nurture or nature will find this journey back easier than those with a cognitive predilection for the Animus.

Jung essentialized these functions to male and female on the assumption of body facticity. However, post-Jungian psychologists view Anima and Animus as archetypes to relate to by individual choice, just like any other archetype. They exist not so much as binary opposites, but upon a spectrum of historically and socially constructed aspects of masculine and feminine. Each end of the spectrum approaches an annihilating infinity of the complete masculine or feminine. On one imagined end is all that is masculine without any input from the feminine. On the other imagined end, is all that is feminine without masculine input, understanding that both ends are absolutes but neither end is absolutely achievable. Human beings are invariably influenced by a confluence of the masculine and feminine to varying degrees of expression. James Hillman views them as paired drives. "Psychic hermaphroditism holds juxtapositions without feeling them as oppositions."[15] Hillman later alludes to a sense of polarity when he argues, "[Hermaphroditus] becomes a Siamese-twin mode of insight. One is always never-only-one, always inseparable bound in a syzygy, insighting from a member of a pair. Within these tandems we become able to reflect insight itself, to regard our own regard. [. . .] [W]hatever appears to me as inferior and weak is viewed from the twin of superiority and strength."[16] The objective of individuation is to bring the Anima and Animus into an androgenic balance, without one dominating the other. According to post-Jungian psychologist June Singer, "Before [male and female energic power] can be joined they must first have been apart, differentiated, separated from one another. Before they were separated, they were bound together in one body, and that body was the Primordial Androgyne."[17] Androgyny is an archetype of the psyche—the point beyond simple masculine and feminine consciousness to which the human mind yearns.[18]

For Jung, the objective of individuation had originally been separation. Jungians have depicted it at times as two overlapping, concentric, black circles that slowly separate over four depictions, the last one showing them completely separated, but still touching at the border and through the axis mundi (ending at Figure 3.1(d)). Taking in the full view of individuation in the light of post-Jungian psychology, incorporating a separation from the Self and an eventual return, the journey of individuation may be depicted as follows in Figure 3.1.

Circles (a) to (d) in Figure 3.1 traditionally depicts individuation as originally conceived in black. In my view, that's been half the story and complete individuation includes depictions of a return. Feminist theorists have also critiqued the androcentric preoccupation with the development of the Ego without due regard for the Ego's desire for connection, which is revealed by circles (d) to (g).[19] The subsequent circles in Figures 3.1(b) through 1(g) show the process of differentiation and reassimilation that occurs through individuation.

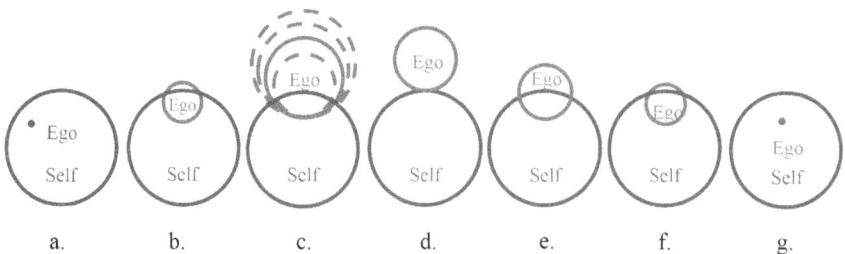

Figure 3.1. Individuation. This figure shows the process of individuation), where the Ego embarks upon a journey of discovery from and to the Self.

Figure 3.2 breaks down the stages of ego separation from birth as a coming-of-age experience, a process Jacobi calls "the crystallization of a stable ego."[20] As such, the Ego is born unaware of any distinction between it and the Self (Figure 3.2(a)). Just as a baby slowly becomes aware of its surroundings, the Ego begins to develop an awareness of the world beyond itself (Figure 3.2(b)). Eventually, the Ego understands that there is a difference between it and the world at large, between consciousness and the unconscious. During this period, a person participates in a period of identity building, at times, over-inflating one's ego until it is properly sized over the course of various life experiences, supported and/or thwarted by the Persona and Shadow (Figure 3.2(c)). The Ego battles its Shadow. In the end, the Ego stabilizes after it assimilates its Shadow, understands its limitations, and realizes that it is not one and the same with the Self (Figure 3.2(d)). At the same time, this level of consciousness brings about a profound sense of absence. The Ego begins to miss the Self that it fought so hard to separate from (Figure 3.3(d)).

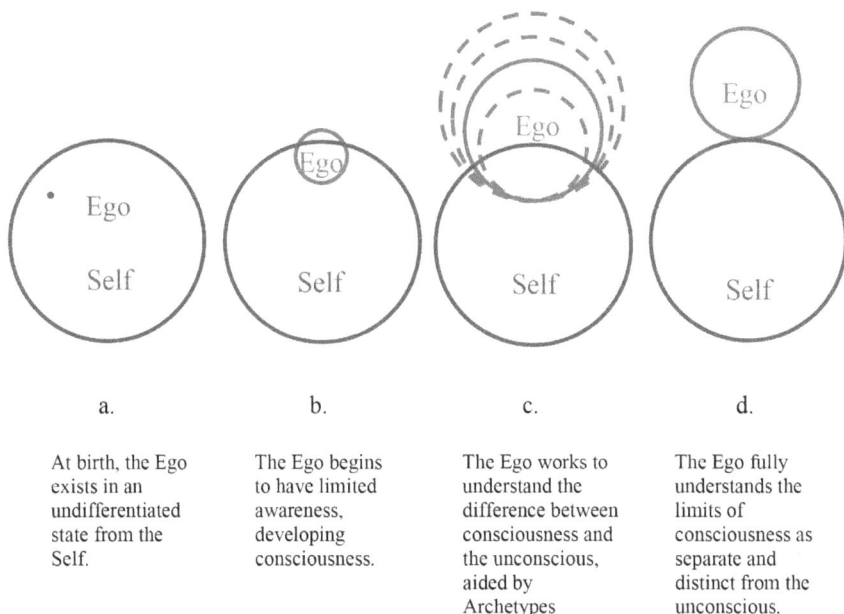

a.	b.	c.	d.
At birth, the Ego exists in an undifferentiated state from the Self.	The Ego begins to have limited awareness, developing consciousness.	The Ego works to understand the difference between consciousness and the unconscious, aided by Archetypes	The Ego fully understands the limits of consciousness as separate and distinct from the unconscious.

Figure 3.2. Coming of Age. This figure shows the process of individuation in the first half of life as a coming of age.

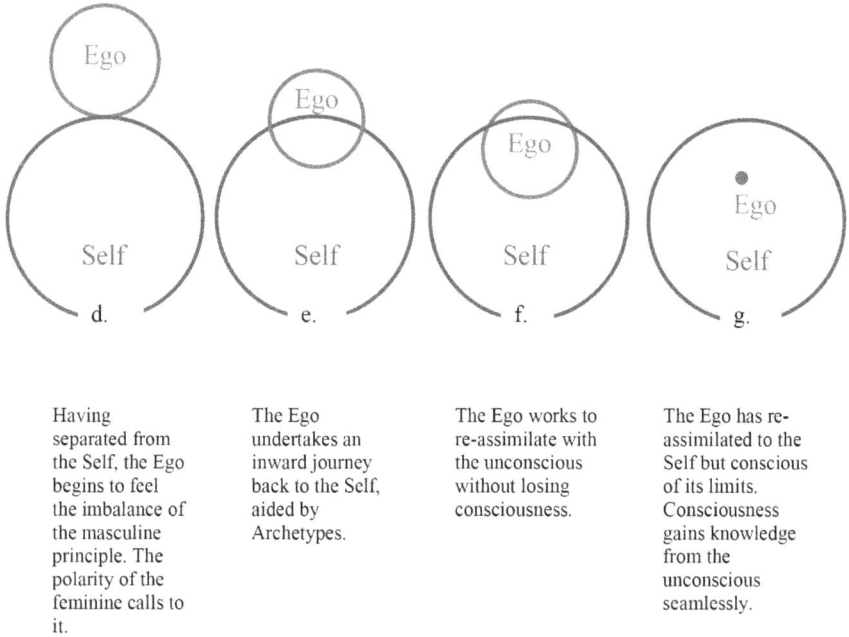

Having separated from the Self, the Ego begins to feel the imbalance of the masculine principle. The polarity of the feminine calls to it.	The Ego undertakes an inward journey back to the Self, aided by Archetypes.	The Ego works to re-assimilate with the unconscious without losing consciousness.	The Ego has re-assimilated to the Self but conscious of its limits. Consciousness gains knowledge from the unconscious seamlessly.

Figure 3.3.   Coming of Middle Age. This figure shows the remaining process of individu-ation, which often occurs later in life as a coming of middle age.

The stages of Ego reintegration with the Self during coming-of-middle-age process are depicted in Figure 3.3. As Jacobi notes:

> At this point the second phase of the individuation process begins when the ego, having become consolidated during the first phase, turns back in order to gather new vitality from contact with its origin, the creative background of the psyche, and to cast anchor in it this time for sure. After having broken away from the domain of the Self, the ego must re-establish a connection with it so as not to remain rootless and lifeless.[21]

Where at birth, a preponderance of feminine energies triggers the masculine principle to call the Ego into active awareness, the overabundance of mascu-line energies that was required to activate consciousness and build a balanced identity in the world prompts a corresponding response from paused feminine energies. The Ego is eager for a reunion with the Self and slowly begins the work back, aided by archetypes often from the underworld (Figure 3.3(e)). By piecemeal, the Ego re-assimilates lost parts of the Self (Figure 3.3(f)), until it's fully re-assimilated into the Self without relinquishing consciousness, which is represented by the Ego maintaining its color on reintegration with the Self in Figure 3.3(g).

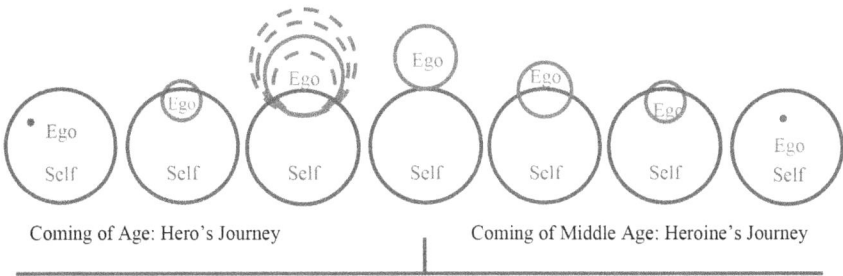

Figure 3.4. The Monomyth Rebooted. This figure superimposes the two journeys of the monomyth over the process of individuation to reveal the interplay between the psychological process of maturation and the character arc drawn from mythological motifs.

Figure 3.4 depicts the monomyth rebooted as both the hero and heroine's journey in individuation.

Where there is a reconciliation in the psyche between the Anima and Animus, there will be a balance between the conscious and unconscious, nature and spirit, heart and soul—a holy marriage of opposites, an *hieros gamos*. Jung refers to the union of the contrasexual archetypes as a syzygy, arguing that this union necessarily incorporates a person's lifetime.[22] The syzygy allows the Ego to know the Self without becoming it. Through individuation culminating in a syzygy, psychic wholeness is achieved. The symbol of psychic wholeness is the birth of a divine child, the simultaneous promise for a bright future and a reminder of what originally was. As a symbol, the divine child "unites the opposites; a mediator, bringer of healing, that is, one who makes whole."[23]

One of the chief mechanisms of public symbolic expression of the archetypes is through myth and mythopoesis. Analytical psychology lends itself as a theoretical framework for mythological studies particularly because Jung and Jungians use myths at times to describe psychological functions. Jung contends that "Myth is the primordial language natural to [. . .] psychic processes, and no intellectual formulation comes anywhere near the richness and expressiveness of mythical imagery."[24] He viewed alchemy as a precursor to modern psychology, with the goal of transforming the psyche from a state of inner division to one of wholeness.[25] Alchemy represents a symbolic process of psychological transformation, through which individuals could integrate their unconscious desires and emotions with their conscious thoughts and actions. Thus, for Jung, alchemy is a spiritual and philosophical tradition that uses symbolism and metaphor to express psychological truths. "What the symbolism of alchemy expresses is the whole problem of the evolution of personality [. . .] the so-called individuation process."[26] Further, post-Jungian psychologist James Hillman refers to the psychologist's tool of "case histories" as representative of "soul stories."[27] Hillman argues that "the soul cannot be understood through [modern] psychology alone."[28] Mythology functions as a guide for comprehending the soul. "To be in touch with the soul means to live in sensuous connection with fantasy."[29] Hillman conceives of fantasy as images of the psyche and mythology as a form of psychology.[30] For mythopoesis, the symbolism of mythology assembled in the monomyth as rebooted in this study represents the entire process of individuation leading to wholeness.

Consequently, in psychological terms, the first half of life focuses on an initiation into adulthood through a hero's journey, separating the Ego from the Self, conquering the Shadow, and identity building. By virtue of its history, the term "hero's journey" implies a male journey, alluding to a passage delimited by sex, when in fact it's a journey accessible by all sexes as a journey of the masculine principle in the first half of life. The second half of life centers on reintegrating with the Self through other archetypes such as the Anima or Animus—what I refer to as the heroine's journey, a quest of that part of the human psyche that carries a constellation of artifacts culturally considered feminine that also needs to grow, mature, and harmonize with those constellations of symbols culturally relegated as masculine. In psychological terms, the latter process does not usually take place until midlife and after a completion of the hero's journey. In storytelling, however, the journeys may be consecutive, concurrent, or independent.

A relevant distinction between the process of individuation and mapping against a mythopoeic structure is a presumption of linearity. For Jung, "There is no linear evolution; there is only a circumambulation of the self. Uniform development exists, at most, only at the beginning; later, everything points towards the center."[31] By virtue of the narrative form, reliant upon language, structure, and logic, storytelling delimits the human experience of individuation to a series of steps. But in reality these steps may be experienced concurrently or one may arrive in advance of the other, or one may take a long time to process while others proceed in quick succession. This perhaps explains Campbell's own late coming conclusion that the monomythic stages of the hero's journey need not all be experienced, may be repeated, or even skipped. A person may be receiving a call to adventure and separating from the mother. Or that person may obtain a boon of success and simultaneously be betrayed. Success can last a short period of time while descent takes years. Or success is repeated, and betrayal happens in an instant. Everyone's process of individuation is unique, and a storyteller at best extrapolates a rational scheme in order to communicate ideas and reach an audience while grasping and holding their imagination through the adoption and subversion of mythological motifs. The following two chapters take a closer look at those steps, first in relation to the hero and then the heroine.

NOTES

1. For a discussion on the Freudian versus Jungian hero in Campbell, see Robert Alan Segal, *Joseph Campbell: An Introduction* (repr. New York: Mentor Books, 1990), 42–53.
2. Jung, "The Archetypes and the Collective Unconscious," 6.
3. C. G. Jung, "*Two Essays on Analytical Psychology*," ed. Herbert Read et al., *The Collected Works of C. G. Jung,* vol. 7 (2nd, Princeton: Princeton University Press, 1966), 173.
4. C. G. Jung, *Psychological Types*, Rev. ed., *The Collected Works of C. G. Jung,* vol. 6, (Princeton: Princeton University Press, 1976).
5. For a discussion on the polarity of the psyche, see Gareth Hill, *Masculine and Feminine: The Natural Flow of Opposites in the Psyche*, 1st ed. (Boston: Shambhala, 1992).
6. Edward F. Edinger, *Ego and Archetype: Individuation and the Religious Runction of the Psyche*, ed. C. G. Jung Foundation for Analytical Psychology (New York: Putnam, 1972), 5.
7. Jolande Jacobi, "The Process of Individuation," *Journal of Analytical Psychology* 111, no. 2 (1958), https://doi.org/10.1111/j.1465-5922.1958.00095.x., pp. 99–100.
8. Jolande Jacobi, *The Way of Individuation* (New York: Harcourt, 1967), 24.
9. C. G. Jung, *The Symbolic Life: Miscellaneous Writings, Collected Works of C. G. Jung*, (Princeton, N.J.: Princeton University Press, 1976), 276.
10. Jung, "The Archetypes and the Collective Unconscious," 58.
11. C. G. Jung, *Man and His Symbols*, ed. Marie-Luise von Franz (Garden City: Doubleday, 1964), 112.
12. C. G. Jung, *Aion: Researches into the Phenomenology of the Self*, ed. Herbert Read et al., 2nd ed., vol. 9, Part 2, *The Collected Works of C.G. Jung*, (Princeton: Princeton University Press, 1968), 8.
13. Jung, *Aion*, 9, Part 2, 20–21.
14. Edward C. Whitmont, *The Symbolic Quest: Basic Concepts of Analytical Psychology*, 2nd ed. (Princeton: Princeton University Press, 1991), 171.
15. Hillman, *Healing Fiction*, 102.
16. Hillman, *Healing Fiction*, 103.
17. June Singer, *Androgyny: Toward a New Theory of Sexuality* (Garden City: Anchor Press, 1976), 21.
18. Hillman argues that this is the perceived "goal of analysis" by Alfred Adler, Sigmeund Freud, and Carl Jung. Hillman, *Healing Fiction*, 102.
19. In the electronic copy of this book, Figures 3.1-3.4 appear in color. The purple, as a composite of red and blue, shows the undifferentiated Ego/Self in 3.1(a), where consciouness and the unconscious are comingled in a hermaphroditic state. The subsequent circles 3.1(b)-(g) highlight the process of differentiation and reassimilation in individuation. Once reintegrated in 3.1(g), the Ego maintains awareness and differentiated as reflected by the red not losing its essence in blue to create purple.
20. Jacobi, *The Way of Individuation*, 64.
21. Jacobi, *The Way of Individuation*, 42.

22. Jung, *Aion*, 9, Part 2, 21, note 5; Edward Edinger, *The Aion Lectures: Exploring the Self in C.G. Jung's Aion* (Toronto: Inner City Books, 1996), 28.

23. Jung, "The Archetypes and the Collective Unconscious," 164.

24. Jung, *Psychology and Alchemy*, 52.

25. Jung, *Psychology and Alchemy*, 54.

26. Jung, *Psychology and Alchemy*, 61.

27. Hillman, *Healing Fiction*, 48.

28. James Hillman, *Re-Visioning Psychology* (New York: Harper Colophon Books, 1977), ix.

29. Hillman, *Re-Visioning Psychology*, 23.

30. Hillman, *Re-Visioning Psychology*, xi and 50.

31. C. G. Jung and Joan Chodorow, *Jung on Active Imagination* (Princeton: Princeton University Press, 1997), 39.

Chapter 4

On the Hero's Journey

A Guide to Christopher Vogler

George Lucas alludes to the impact of *The Hero with a Thousand Faces* on *Star Wars* when he proclaimed that Joseph Campbell was his mentor. Despite problematic propositions presented in the monomyth, storytellers have nonetheless made use of its unproblematic mythological motifs. Christopher Vogler edited the monomyth into a functioning, modern, user-friendly mythic structure for writers to adopt, simplified it to a twelve-step hero's journey, and proved that it worked against story in *The Writer's Journey*. Hollywood accepted this abridged version as Campbellian canon. The monomyth and the hero's journey became synonymous. Three stories in which the hero's journey can be found complete are Eros and Psyche, *Jane Eyre*, and *Titanic*.[1]

ORDINARY WORLD: STEP ONE

Vogler begins by splitting Campbell's first step into two separate steps with the hero's home base and then a call to adventure. The hero's journey begins in the Ordinary World, where he is shown at home in his everyday life going about his usual routine.[2] This may introduce backstory, provide a prologue, foreshadow, state the theme, or exhibit the hero's flaw or conflict. It is a contrasting world to the one in his future. Joseph Campbell uses the Brothers Grimm fairy tale, the "Frog King" or "Iron Heinrich," as an initial example of the call—a tale about a prince who'd been cursed into an amphibious form to live in a deep, bottomless well but told by projection onto a princess, described as more beautiful than the sun. While Campbell explores this from the princess's perspective, a hero's journey reveals itself in the eponymous character. The princess frolics far into the dark forest by her father's castle, where she likes to sit by the well under an old linden tree. In mythology, the linden tree is sacred. In German mythology, it's seen as the tree of truth and alternatively the lovers' tree. In Greek mythology, Baucis and Philemon, an old married couple who were the only ones to welcome Zeus and Hermes into their home when the gods disguised themselves as mendicants, were memorialized as two intertwining trees, an oak and a linden, upon their deaths. Beneath this tree the princess plays with a golden ball, while the proteus at the bottom of the well, lives out a waterlogged life in the darkness of his Ordinary World.

The myth of Eros and Psyche assumes on the reader an understanding of Eros from the corpus of Greek and Roman mythology, where he is also known as Cupid or Amor. He is the mischievous god of love, equipped with two kinds of arrows, a lead-tipped one to dampen love and a golden-tipped one to fuel it. His victims will either become happy in love or pine forever for love lost, as in the case of Apollo who angered Eros and was shot with a golden arrow to fall in love with the water nymph Daphne, whom he shot with a leaden arrow. She successfully escapes Apollo's amorous pursuits when she appeals to her father to turn her into a laurel tree.

More often than not, Eros is seen destroying a couple rather than joining them together. His mother, Aphrodite, the goddess of beauty, describes him as that "winged headstrong boy, that wicked boy, scorner of law and order, who, armed with arrows and torch aflame, speeds through others' homes by night, saps the ties of wedlock, and all unpunished commits hideous crime and uses all his power for ill."[3] Therefore, to begin, Eros has yet to give up a hedonistic lifestyle and grow into a man.

In *Jane Eyre*, by Charlotte Brontë, Jane is a ten-year old orphan living in her deceased uncle's home, as an unwanted, and at times, despised relation. In her Ordinary World, she lives as an inferior to her three cousins, forced to take miserable, cold walks in the winter while they sat nestled by a fire where she was unwelcome. Jane says,

> [Her aunt] regretted to be under the necessity of keeping me at a distance; but that until she heard from Bessie and could discover by her own observation that I was endeavoring in good earnest to acquire a more sociable and childlike disposition, a more attractive and spritely manner—something lighter, franker, more natural, as it were—she really must exclude me from privileges intended only for contented, happy, little children.[4]

Jane busies herself with reading, conscious to simultaneously avoid her menacing cousin, John Reed, four years her senior and constantly bullying and physically abusing her.

In *Titanic*, directed by James Cameron, Jack Dawson is an artist who lives as free as a tumbleweed, letting chance direct the course of his life. He comes onto the scene as a cherubic figure, his first name being the diminutive of

John, which itself derives from the Hebrew Yohanan, meaning *God is gracious*. In Arabic, his name means the enlivener. Jack also represents a cupid character because his last name is Dawson, which means the son of David—a Biblical reference to the second king of Israel but also meaning *the beloved.*[5] In his Ordinary World, he wins third-class tickets on the Titanic for himself and his friend, gambling and gamboling through life.

Call to Adventure: Step Two

The Call to Adventure is the second step in Vogler's iteration of the hero's journey, where the hero may be summoned, beguiled, tempted, heralded, chased, triggered, or forced into an escapade, willingly or unwillingly. The Call to Adventure in story can be represented by a messenger, coincidences, character disorientation, temptation, loss, need, changes, or self-defense. Using Campbell's example of the "Frog King," the call begins when an auriferous globe falls out of the sky and into amphibious waters, creating small waves. This is the call to consciousness. The Ego must arise and understand the bright, exciting world. The Ego is depicted in the shape of an ugly "water-splasher," who hears the princess crying over her lost ball. He agrees to help the princess retrieve her possession in exchange for companionship to which she assents.

In Eros and Psyche, Eros's adventure begins with a summons from his mother, Aphrodite, to avenge her for losing her status as the most worshipped to Psyche. Aphrodite needs him to do away with Psyche—the young, captivating princess venerated by her father's subjects—cast her on a mountain, and compel her to fall in love with a monster. In that way, Aphrodite would be rid of the threat to her own incomparable beauty. She leads him directly to Psyche for closer inspection. Trusting the problem to the destructive hands of her son who was adept at committing crimes with impunity, Aphrodite retreats to her water world.

In *Jane Eyre*, Jane responds to the call by standing up for herself against the violence being inflicted upon her by her cousin. After one particularly bloody incident, she strikes back.

> He ran headlong at me: I felt him grasp my hair and my shoulder: he had closed with a desperate thing. I really saw in him a tyrant: a murderer. I felt a drop or two of blood from my head trickle down my neck, and was sensible of somewhat pungent suffering: these sensations for the time predominated over fear, and I received him in a frantic sort. I don't very well know what I did with my hands, but he called me 'Rat! Rat!' and bellowed out aloud.[6]

In *Titanic*, Jack's Call to Adventure occurs when he stumbles upon Rose attempting to take her own life. He's either going to help her or watch her die. For him, there's no option but to prevent that catastrophe. He quickly follows her to the stern flagpole, where she stares into the inviting ocean, and he says, "Don't do it."[7]

Refusal of the Call: Step Three

Like Joseph Campbell, Vogler argues that the next step of the hero's journey is a Refusal of the Call. At this point, the hero may waver in his commitment, find the call too dangerous, or need to weigh the consequences. In psychological terms, the Ego refuses to separate from the comfort of the Self. The refusal can be depicted by avoidance, excuses, receiving conflicting calls, expressing doubts, threshold guardians blocking the way, or the refusal by someone in the hero's surrounds. His friends may try to convince him to reconsider and turn back. In the "Frog King," right after the frog fulfills his part of the bargain, the princess refuses the call by snubbing her end of the bargain. With ball in hand, she runs back home and away from the odious frog.

In Eros and Psyche, Aphrodite summons the "scorner of law and order," anticipating Eros's headstrong mind of refusal.[8] Eros ultimately refuses his mother's call to destroy Psyche in having her fall in love with a monster. Enrapt by her beauty, he has her fall in love with him instead. He commands the West Wind to carry her off to his home, where she becomes his bride. In *Jane Eyre*, Jane begins to have doubts once she's imprisoned in her uncle's bedroom and her anger subsides. As darkness settles in her jail, "My habitual mood of humiliation, self-doubt, forlorn depression, fell damp on the embers of my decaying ire."[9] Jane reverts to hopelessness, eventually passing out, unable to bear the weight of the consequences. In *Titanic*, Jack is met with a refusal of the call from Rose's threshold guardian and fiancé, Cal, and the Master at Arms, who handcuffs Jack, while Cal says, "What made you think you could put your hands on my fiancé?! Look at me, you filth!"[10]

Meeting with the Mentor: Step Four

In the fourth step of the hero's journey, the hero Meets with the Mentor, a step that Vogler adapts and widens from Joseph Campbell's Supernatural Aid. The mentor protects, tests, guides, and provides magical gifts. He or she or they may not be an actual person or persons, but may be a thing, such as a book, map, computer—a source of guidance or journey aid in any event. Mentors inspire the hero with courage to enter the unknown zone before them, and they can be alive or dead. In the "Frog King," the princess's father steps in to scold his daughter for dishonoring her agreement with the frog, thereby protecting the frog and mentoring his daughter to right action.

In Eros and Psyche, Eros is mentored by his mother, Aphrodite, as "the first parent of created things, the primal source of all the elements."[11] She gives him the mission and then "with parted lips, kissed her son long and fervently."[12] In Greco-Roman mythology, spit is used in magical spells to prevent impotence.[13] In ancient Taoist lore, female saliva is one of the three yin great medicines that activates a man's five senses and increases his vital essence.[14] In medieval Jewish, Christian, and Islamic traditions, spittle is imbued with curative, protective powers used in white or black magic, for or against evil.[15] Thus, Aphrodite arms Eros with a safeguarding talisman for his quest.

In *Jane Eyre*, Jane is mentored by the apothecary, Mr. Lloyd, who treats her for a concussion and malnourishment. "I felt an inexpressible relief, a soothing conviction of protection and security, when I knew that there was a stranger in the room [. . .]."[16] She then feels dismayed at his departure. "I felt so sheltered and befriended while he sat in the chair near my pillow; and as he closed the door after him all the room darkened and my heart again sank: inexpressible sadness weighed it down."[17] Mr. Lloyd takes the time to understand Jane and allows her to vent her frustrations. He realizes that the solution to her predicament would be boarding school and convinces Mrs. Reed to let her attend.

In *Titanic*, once Cal realizes that Jack saved Rose, he invites him to dinner in first class. Molly Brown mentors Jack because "[he's] about to go into the snake pit."[18] She helps him dress the part of a gentleman by giving him her son's new suit, advising and arming him with the requisite accoutrements to surprise and disarm his hosts.

Crossing the First Threshold: Step Five

The fifth step in the hero's journey is Crossing the First Threshold, a stage taken from Campbell but elucidated by Vogler. Hero has reached a point of no return and commits wholeheartedly to the adventure. He enters a no man's land. In psychological terms, the Ego embarks on separating from the Self, beginning to understand that it and the Self are not one and the same. This stage is marked by threshold guardians blocking the way, a borderland between worlds, or a rough landing of some sort, where there is evidence that the crossing is not easy but exhausting, frustrating, or disorienting. It may require a leap of faith across any kind of gateway—bridges, canyons, walls, cliffs, oceans, rivers, or space. In the "Frog King," the frog chases after the princess who reneged on their pact, crossing the marble staircase of the castle courtyard, a no-man's land, to knock on her door. When at the King's insistence, the princess opens the palatial entrance, the frog enters a no-frog land to sit by the princess.

In Eros and Psyche, Eros sends the West Wind to carry Psyche away from the mountain and into the valley, where he has a castle. Unbeknownst to her, she enters a no-mortal land, paved with gemstones leading to gold columns and a roof carved in sandalwood and ivory. "Allured by the charm and beauty of the place, Psyche drew near and, as her confidence increased, crossed the threshold."[19]

Prior to her matriculation at Lowood Institution, Jane meets its director, Mr. Brocklehurst, the threshold guardian who castigates her as a naughty child. She dramatically departs from her home, declaring to no one, "Good-bye to Gateshead! cried I, as we passed through the hall and went out at the front door."[20] In the middle of the night, she takes a coach for a "preternatural length" during which "we ceased to pass through towns; the country changed; great grey hills heaved up round the horizon: as twilight deepened we descended a valley, dark with wood, and long after night had overclouded the prospect I heard a wild wind rushing amongst trees."[21] Finally when they reached their destination, "Rain, wind, and darkness filled the air; nevertheless, I dimly discerned a wall before me and a door open in it; through this door I passed with my new guide: she shut and locked it behind her. [. . .] [W]e went up a broad pebbly path, splashing wet, and were admitted at a door; then the servant led me through a passage into a room with a fire, where she left me alone."[22]

Penniless Jack has been invited to dinner with the wealthiest members of society. A steward guards the doorway to the A-Deck reception room and lets Jack through, the same threshold guardian who will deny him entrance on the morrow. He enters a sphere unlike any he's been in before, with a glass dome ceiling and crystal chandelier suspended over a grand staircase. Rose escorts him, showing him around and pointing out all the notables in the set, where he's soon mistaken for one.

Tests, Allies, and Enemies: Step Six

Vogler's sixth step of the hero's journey is Tests, Allies, and Enemies, taken from Campbell's section on the Road of Trials, which skips over Campbell's Belly of the Whale. According to Campbell, in this phase hero must survive a series of trials in a dreamlike, fluid landscape. It's a new, special world, in contrast to the ordinary world, wherethe hero makes friends and enemies while learning new rules. This stage is often depicted at a common gathering place, where the hero gains information and resources. In psychological terms, the hero may be over-identifying with his persona archetype and discovering his shadows. In the "Frog King," the frog has gained the companionship of the princess and sits at the dinner table with her. From her perspective, he is a grotesque enemy.

In Eros and Psyche, Eros has made Psyche his wife, under the condition that she not gaze upon him. While he leaves during the day, she grows lonely and wishes to spend time with her sisters, but Eros perceives them as her enemy and warns her against them. Eventually, Eros relents and allows her sisters to visit, having the West Wind deliver them. The sisters grow jealous at Psyche's wealth and happiness. By subsequent visits, they plot against her, planting seeds of doubt in her mind about her husband, who was probably still a monster, since she's never seen him and threatens her with dire consequences should she do so, while Eros continues to warn her especially since she's become pregnant. The sisters' machinations lead to their untimely death but not without successfully convincing Psyche that for her own good she must kill the serpent she's wed to. The sisters represent friends who become her enemies, and Psyche is tried by misgivings she has about her husband.

Jane Eyre begins a new life at a new school. It's a special world compared to her previous one, an irregular building with compartment after compartment, like a maze. She meets Miss Miller, the only teacher to treat her with kindness, and is immediately led into the dining hall full of students, where she has dinner. Jane must learn the rules of Lowood, where to assemble, where to sit, when to speak, what to wear, what chores to do, when to play, when to sleep, when to pray, and when to learn, all signaled by the ringing of a bell. "My first quarter at Lowood seemed an age; and not the golden age either: it comprised an irksome struggle with difficulties in habituating myself to new rules and unwonted tasks. The fear of failure in these points harassed me worse than the physical hardships of my lot; though these were no trifles,"[23] because they were consistently hungry and underdressed for the elements. She befriends her classmate, Helen, who teaches her about the school. When she finds Helen reading *Rasselas*, a philosophical novel proving that happiness cannot be found on earth, she flips through it and dismisses it as uninteresting, foreshadowing each of their respective challenges with happiness.

Jack's road of trials begins in the dining room, where he dines with high society. From across the table, Rose gestures to take his napkin off his plate, quietly instructing him on proper etiquette. When he reaches for a fish fork to eat salad, Rose hints with her eyes to pick up the salad utensil. He is tried before a jury of the peerless to account for the accommodations in steerage, living a rootless life, and eschewing caviar. He explains to his audience that he believes in making every day count, leaving Rose a note to meet him at the clock of Honor and Glory, a nod to the theme of the *Iliad* in which honor and glory survive a hero's death, making him legendary, and foreshadowing a future date with that clock. He takes her down to the third-class dining hall that looks more like a tavern and dance hall, where Rose becomes one of the guys. Jack gains Rose's friendship while making enemies of Cal and the steward.

Approach to the Inmost Cave: Step Seven

The seventh step of the hero's journey is marked by an Approach to the Inmost Cave, representing the penultimate struggle of the hero, which further draws from Campbell's original Road of Trials. Hero's new skills and lessons are tested. He may pause to regroup, strategize, prepare, give or heed warnings, fight against patriarchy, enter a shamanic region, feel a false sense of security, make a breakthrough, or pierce a veil. This step establishes high stakes for the forthcoming Ordeal. It can be represented as a mini-special world, an initial threshold and final threshold, or complications in reaching the cave. It may also be reflected in an awkward romance, courtship, or more threshold guardians. In the "Frog King," after dinner, the frog wishes to sleep, having grown weary with fatigue. The princess, as a threshold guardian, reluctantly picks him up with two fingers and carries him to her room, dumping him in a corner, where he feels a false sense of security in a mini-special world of the castle.

Eros and Psyche have a moment of awkward romance. Psyche now fearful of whom she married, plots to kill her husband once he falls asleep. "Now it was night, and her husband had come; after a short skirmish of lovemaking, he fell fast asleep,"[24] completely oblivious to the concerns and worries of his wife for having forced her to love him in the dark. Jane Eyre approaches the inmost cave when Mr. Brocklehurst arrives for inspection, the threshold guardian returning for further condemnations. It takes her a while to share his first visit because it took him a while to make it. Up until that time, she lived in false security. "I have not yet alluded to the visits of Mr. Brocklehurst; and indeed that gentleman was from home during the greater part of the first month after my arrival; perhaps prolonging his stay with his friend the archdeacon: his absence was a relief to me."[25] He is the patriarchy she's avoiding, using her slate as a shield to hide behind. But there was no escaping his recriminations.

In the *Titanic*, Jack tries to see Rose the next day after dinner and is met with the same steward threshold guardian, refusing him entrance. Jack's no longer welcome in first class. But Jack sneaks back up and grabs Rose's attention for a brief moment of awkward courtship, by pulling her into the mini-special world of the first class gymnasium. She insists that she can't see him, but he insists that he's too involved not to care about her welfare. He's worried that she will be imprisoned in her life. "You're goin' to die if you don't break out,"[26] he says. She begs him to leave her alone.

Ordeal: Step Eight

The eighth step of the hero's journey is the Ordeal, what Campbell refers to earlier in the process as the Belly of the Whale but marking a judicious edit by Vogler to delay it, for this is the stage of the ultimate struggle where hero faces his greatest fear. In psychological terms, hero must slay an inflated Ego by conquering (thereby assimilating) his shadow. In story, this is depicted by an experience of death: an end to a relationship, a villain, an ally, or even the hero, who appears to die. There could be a crisis of the heart or conflict between past and present, old and new, young and old. This stage is symbolized by a whiff of death, especially if it takes place in a dark, inhospitable, foreign place, such as a cavern. In the "Frog King," the frog insists on sleeping with the princess on her bed—the most inhospitable site. This pushes the princess to her limits, where she then picks up the frog and flings him against the wall, trying to kill him. In essence, she succeeds (whiff of death) because he miraculously transforms into a handsome prince, having shed his amphibious self.

Psyche takes the lamp to shed light in the darkened recess of their bedroom to finally gaze upon her sleeping husband and discovers him to be a beautiful god, regretting her previous intentions to kill him instantaneously. She finds his arrows and unintentionally pierces herself, falling in love with Love. This compels her to "cast herself upon him in an ecstasy of love, heap[ing] wanton kiss on kiss with thirsty hastening lips,"[27] which results in her accidentally spilling lamp oil on him, seriously injuring him. Eros awakes to a state of betrayal. He's been exposed, all of his secrets have been stripped bare. He flies away, but she grabs onto his heel until she can hold on no longer, falling to her death but landing safely on earth instead. He flies to a nearby cypress, accusing her of untoward, treacherous behavior, ignoring the fact that he placed an unreasonable burden of blindness on their love. Her punishment is his disappearance and abandonment.

Jane's Ordeal begins when she accidentally drops and breaks her slate, calling Mr. Brocklehurst's attention to her and the economic loss she just created. In front of all the teachers and students, he demands that she stand on a stool in the middle of the room, where he denounces her as a liar to be shunned. Jane is utterly humiliated before her peers and mentors. She's left alone in silence and darkness for her punishment at the end of which she collapses to the floor in tears. "[H]ere I lay again crushed and trodden on; and could I ever rise more?

'Never,' I thought and ardently I wished to die."[28] This is a moment of metaphorical death for Jane.

Rose changes her mind about Jack and asks him to draw her wearing only the Heart of the Ocean. This requires Jack to enter the inmost cave of her room. His Ordeal is to steal all the moments he can with her, without getting caught. He appears nervous, dropping his pencil and blushing. Despite his experience as an artist, he's a novice at love. When they're finished, Rose writes Cal a note, effectively ending their engagement. Jack has to sneak back to steerage while escaping the watchful eye of Cal's bodyguard and a mad dash with Rose to the belly of the ship to save his life ensues.

Reward: Step Nine

The ninth step of the hero's journey is the Reward, where hero gains the prize or seizes the sword. This usually results in scenes of celebrating, campfire gatherings, lovemaking, or coming to new realizations. In the "Frog Prince,' the prince marries the princess, by edict of the king. For Eros, his reward is realizing the full length of the betrayal and his own stupidity.

> I forgot the commands of my mother [Aphrodite], who bade me fire thee with passion for some miserable abject man and yoke thee in wedlock to him, and myself flew to thy side that I might be thy lover in his place. But this I did thoughtlessly, as now I know. For I, the far-famed archer, wounded myself with my own shafts, and made thee my bride to win this reward—that thou shouldst deem me a wild beast, and shouldst hew off my head with blade of steel, that head where dwell these eyes that love thee so dearly.[29]

He also promises vengeance against the sisters that plotted against them.

Jane is helped by Helen to come to a better understanding of her plight. "God waits only the separation of spirit from flesh to crown us with a full reward. Why, then, should we ever sink overwhelmed with distress, when life is so soon over, and death is so certain an entrance to happiness—to glory," Helen says. Later, Miss Temple invites Jane and Helen to tea, allowing Jane to defend herself against Mr. Brocklehurst's charges which later exonerates her. And then:

> We feasted that evening on nectar and ambrosia; and not the least delight of the entertainment was the smile of gratification with which our hostess regarded us, as we satisfied our famished appetites on the delicate fare she liberally supplied. Tea over and the tray removed, she again summoned us to the fire; we sat one on each side of her, and now a conversation followed between her and Helen, which it was indeed a privilege to be admitted to hear.[30]

Jane is Rewarded with new insights and a celebratory feast.

Jack is Rewarded for his Ordeal with lovemaking, where it seems this could be Jack's first time. Afterwards, Rose tells him that when they dock in

America, she wants to go with him. He's won the love of his life, the love of a lifetime.

Road Back: Step Ten

In the tenth step of the hero's journey, the hero embarks on the Road Back, which is synthesized from Campbell's Refusal of the Return, Magic Flight, and Crossing the Return Threshold, where hero may be seen on the road of return that includes a renewed threat by the villain, a sounding of the alarm, pulling together as a team or family especially after death, hot-pursuits, reversals of fortune, magical escapes, a reminder of the ultimate goal, or simply a period of rest that the hero may be unwilling to relinquish. In the "Frog King," the next morning the prince becomes king—a reminder of his ultimate goal—and his faithful servant Heinrich appears with an imperial carriage led by eight horses crowned in ostrich feathers and harnessed in gold for a charmed return to his kingdom.

Psyche seeks the support of her devious sisters, guilelessly explaining to them what had happened and how Eros tossed her out on the promise of replacing her with her sisters. This was Eros's ruse to incite the sisters to pursue him to their own destruction, where each in turn left her husband and quickly flung themselves down the mountain on the dashed expectation that the West Wind would carry them to Eros. The sisters presented a renewed threat, which Eros deftly handled at a distance, reversing their fortunes by their own greed. In the meantime, needing to heal his wound, Eros flies back to his mother who suddenly discovers that he had betrayed her request. His mother threatens to strip him of his powers as punishment and then enlists the help of her enemy, Sobriety, to do just that. Sobriety slashes his golden locks, blunts his arrows, extinguishes his torch, and clips his wings. This is a setback for Eros during his recuperation. In the meantime, his mother has given Psyche four impossible tasks, which he magically and indirectly helps her with by the reverence all creatures show him in coming to his wife's aid.

Having been vindicated, Jane settles more comfortably into her life at Lowood, until the spring brings an epidemic, turning the school into an infirmary of the sick. In this time, Jane makes a new friend and roams the property a little more freely while everyone else is in the hospital, sick, or tending to the sick. For a while, she reaches a plateau of comfort, unwilling to become aware of a single truth—her best friend is dying.

> I lingered yet a little longer: the flowers smelt so sweet as the dew fell; it was such a pleasant evening, so serene, so warm; the still glowing west promised so fairly another fine day on the morrow; the moon rose with such majesty in the grave east. I was noting these things and enjoying them as a child might, when it

entered my mind as it had never done before:—"How sad to be lying now on a
sick bed, and to be in danger of dying! This world is pleasant it would be dreary
to be called from it, and to have to go who knows where?"[31]

This is a sounding of the alarm brought on by an unnamed external force Jane
overhears.

The *Titanic* ship suffers a setback when it hits an iceberg. Jack's future
outlook with Rose suddenly reverses when Cal accuses him of stealing the
Heart of the Ocean, which metaphorically he had stolen the heart of Cal's
ocean, Rose's love. But in actuality, Cal planted the necklace to be discovered
in Jack's pocket right in front of Rose, which causes her to doubt him. Jack is
arrested for theft and handcuffed to a pipe in the Master of Arms Office in the
lower level of the ship. Everything he gained was lost, including his freedom.

Resurrection: Step Eleven

Resurrection is the eleventh step of the hero's journey, a confluence of
Campbell's Rescue from Without and Crossing of the Return Threshold,
with touches of Supernatural Aid from Magic Flight. In story, this stage is
depicted by a second ordeal, a showdown, a difficult choice, an emotional
breakthrough, a catharsis, a sacrifice, spiritual cleansing, sacred rituals, a
near-death experience, a rebirth, shared treasures, or a material change in
hero's character. In the "Frog King," Heinrich, the king's servant has a catharsis when the iron bands clasping his heart break open—iron bands that had
encircled him to prevent his heart from bursting with grief when the prince
had originally disappeared under the cloud of the curse.

Once Eros has healed, he's able to fly to Psyche, who has fallen into a deep
sleep, and resurrect her with a prick of his arrow. This allows her to continue
her duties to his mother, while he ascends to the heavens for a meeting with
Zeus in sacred space. There he is called to confession and cleansed of past
misdeeds. As a consequence, he becomes a man when Zeus proclaims, "the
wanton spirit of boyhood must be enchained in the fetters of wedlock."[32]

Jane rushes to Helen's bedside when she realizes that Helen is dying of
tuberculosis. They speak of being reunited in heaven, and Jane hugs her all
through the night. Helen dies in her arms and is buried in an unmarked grave
of the churchyard until Jane later places a marble gravestone on it with the
word "Resurgam," Latin for "I shall rise again"[33]—a promise of resurrection.

Jack and Rose face an incredible physical ordeal of escaping imprisonment
and a sinking ship. They are successful in the latter but not the former. They
go down with the ship, but both miraculously resurface in a dual resurrection.
As they float in the icy waters, Jack sacrifices himself to safeguard Rose on
a floating door.

Return with the Elixir: Step Twelve

Return with the Elixir is Vogler's twelfth and final step, taking elements from Campbell's Ultimate Boon and Freedom to Live. In psychological terms, the Ego has emerged from the Self, identifying with his Persona and his Shadow in their proper perspectives, as archetypes to draw knowledge from, not to be subsumed by. The Ego is no longer inflated. In the "Frog King," the Return with the Elixir is demonstrated when the last band caging Heinrich's heart breaks. The king's rightful return heals him of the tightness in his chest.

Eros is rewarded with a heavenly marriage to Psyche, who is offered the elixir of ambrosia that turns her into a god, solidifying their union as eternal. At last, "The bridegroom reclined on the couch of honor holding Psyche to his heart."[34] After Helen's death, an investigation is launched into the conditions of the school, and due to public indignation, a new school is built, Brocklehurst is replaced, and healthier policies are implemented. Jane lives a contented life, edifying her mind and gaining skills which enables her to be promoted to teacher.

> During these eight years my life was uniform: but not unhappy, because it was not inactive. I had the means of an excellent education placed within my reach. A fondness for some of my studies, and a desire to excel in all, together with a great delight in pleasing my teachers, especially such as I loved, urged me on: I availed myself fully of the advantages offered me. In time I rose to be the first girl of the first class; then I was invested with the office of teacher; which I discharged with zeal for two years [. . .].[35]

Jack's elixir is the love he shares with Rose for which he is grateful. He extracts a promise from her to live life to its fullest before he sinks into a watery grave. His physical form dies, but he is immortalized by their love as referenced in the film's theme song, "My Heart Will Go On." At the end, they share a heavenly union when they are reunited at Rose's death, which takes place after she fulfills her promise to him.

What was once difficult for Campbell to prove, Vogler achieves by streamlining the monomyth in such a way as to establish a pattern that exists in story across genre and time. Because Campbell concluded that deletion and/or re-arrangement of steps was a necessary part of the monomyth, the hero's journey remains a kind of example of the hero with a thousand faces. However, Vogler's deletion of five steps elided the monomyth of salient features of mythic quests. Vogler's defects are cured by an altogether different arrangement of Campbell's steps—a heroine's journey.

NOTES

1. I approach the analysis of these stories in this section from a monomythic perspective, but I note that Eros and Psyche has been analyzed from a psychological perspective. See Erich Neumann, *Amor and Psyche: The Psychic Development of the Feminine, a Commentary on the Tale by Apuleius*, trans. Ralph Manheim (repr. Princeton: Princeton University Press, 1971); Marie-Louise von Franz, *The Golden Ass of Apuleius: The Liberation of the Feminine in Man*, rev. ed. (Boston: Shambhala Publications, 1992); Ulanov, *The Feminine in Jungian Psychology and in Christian Theology*; James Hillman, *The Myth of Analysis: Three Essays in Archetypal Psychology* (Evanston: Northwestern University Press, 1972); Murray Stein and Lionel Corbett, eds., *Psyche's Stories: Modern Jungian Interpretations of Fairy Tales*, 3 vols., vol. 1 (Wilmette: Chiron Publications, 1995); Robert A. Johnson, *She: Understanding Feminine Psychology*, rev. ed. (New York: Perennial Library, 1989).

2. The pronouns used mirror the psychic principle of the journey. The hero's journey is a journey of the masculine principle of the mind as reflected by he/him. The heroine's journey, as the journey of the feminine principle of the mind is followed by pronouns of she/her. Both psychic journeys are traveled by all genders.

3. Lucius Apuleius, *The Metamorphoses, or Golden Ass of Apuleius of Madaura*, trans. Harold Edgeworth Butler, 2 vols. (Oxford: Clarendon Press, 1910), 128–29.

4. Charlotte Brontë, *Jane Eyre* (repr. New York, London: Harper, 1899), 1.

5. Patrick Hanks, Kate Hardcastle, and Flavia Hodges, *A Dictionary of First Names*, ed. Kate Hardcastle and Flavia Hodges, 2nd ed., Oxford Reference, (Oxford & New York: Oxford University Press, 2006), 71.

6. Brontë, *Jane Eyre*, 6.

7. James Cameron, *Titanic: James Cameron's Illustrated Screenplay* (New York: HarperPerennial, 1998), 61.

8. Apuleius, *The Metamorphoses, or Golden Ass of Apuleius of Madaura*, 127.

9. Brontë, *Jane Eyre*, 12.

10. Cameron, *Screenplay*, 36.

11. Apuleius, *The Metamorphoses, or Golden Ass of Apuleius of Madaura*, 128.

12. Apuleius, *The Metamorphoses, or Golden Ass of Apuleius of Madaura*, 129.

13. Daniel Ogden, *Magic, Witchcraft, and Ghosts in the Greek and Roman worlds: A Sourcebook* (Oxford; New York: Oxford University Press, 2002), 264.

14. Fangfu Ruan and Molleen Matsumura, *Sex in China: Studies in Sexology in Chinese Culture* (New York: Plenum Press, 1991), 84.

15. For a general discussion on sacred saliva, see Adam Collins Bursi, "Holy Spit and Magic Spells: Religion, Magic, and the Body in late Ancient Judaism, Christianity, and Islam," (PhD diss., Cornell University, 2015).

16. Brontë, *Jane Eyre*, 15.

17. Brontë, *Jane Eyre*, 16.

18. Cameron, *Screenplay*, 52.

19. Apuleius, *The Metamorphoses, or Golden Ass of Apuleius of Madaura*, 135.

20. Brontë, *Jane Eyre*, 43.

21. Brontë, *Jane Eyre*, 43.

22. Brontë, *Jane Eyre*, 44–45.

23. Brontë, *Jane Eyre*, 66.

24. Apuleius and Sarah Ruden, *The Golden Ass* (New Haven Conn.: Yale University Press, 2011), 106.

25. Brontë, *Jane Eyre*, 68.

26. Brontë, *Jane Eyre*, 69.

27. Apuleius, *The Metamorphoses, or Golden Ass of Apuleius of Madaura*, 152.

28. Brontë, *Jane Eyre*, 77.

29. Apuleius, *The Metamorphoses, or Golden Ass of Apuleius of Madaura*, 153.

30. Brontë, *Jane Eyre*, 82–83.

31. Brontë, *Jane Eyre*, 90.

32. Apuleius, *The Metamorphoses, or Golden Ass of Apuleius of Madaura*, 180.

33. "Resurgam, phr.," OED Online, December 2020, Oxford University Press, https://www-oed-com.proxy.library.georgetown.edu/view/Entry/164092?redirectedFrom=resurgam& (accessed February 27, 2021).

34. Apuleius, *The Metamorphoses, or Golden Ass of Apuleius of Madaura*, 181.

35. Brontë, *Jane Eyre*, 97.

Chapter 5

On the Heroine's Journey

A Post-Murdock Approach

Maureen Murdock uncovered a psychological pattern occurring in midlife that can be found in mythology and tracked in mythopoesis in *The Heroine's Journey, A Woman's Guide for Wholeness*.[1] Applying to both men and women, the journey is triggered by an estrangement from a maternal figure, reflecting the initial moment the Ego disengages from the Self and subsequently signals the individuated Ego back to the Self. As a result of separation, the heroine overidentifies with the masculine until she sets out on her own path to experience a series of trials. Once successful in her tests, she gains awards and accolades until she realizes that they were illusory. She feels betrayed and plunges into a depression that could last years. Climbing out of that requires reconnection with nature and creativity until she is strong enough to confront the maternal and heal the mother/child divide. Once she accomplishes that, she must heal the wounded masculine within her. This allows her to unite the feminine and masculine aspects of her psyche in a psychic harmony. Murdock's approach gynocentrically focuses on women securing wholeness. As part of a lived life, the stages are not expected to begin and end successively. Rather, some may continue as others begin. Some may even be revisited whilst in the midst others.

This discussion scrutinizes Murdock's theory by parsing through the psychological phases more specifically for its mythopoeic signposts. My arguments extends the discourse on the heroine's journey by elaborating upon specific stages, thereby addressing the previously unexplored lacunas. Murdock posits that women undergo a phase of descent. In terms of mythopoesis, given the temporal breadth of such a descent, I bifurcated this process into two distinct stages: the act of descending and the subsequent dwelling within the descent. Murdock also summarily integrates the masculine and the feminine in one chapter. Within narrative structures, this process unfolds through three distinct phases: firstly, the association with a good man; secondly, the act of union; and finally, the ensuing state of bliss. Consequently, this culminates in a twelve-step sequence for the heroine's journey as an integral component of the monomyth reboot, which I scrutinize in correlation with the same triad of narratives previously examined for the hero's journey, Eros and Psyche, *Jane Eyre*, and *Titanic*. Finally, all references to "heroine" denote a person, irrespective of gender, undertaking a coming-of-middle-age, künstlerroman, where "middle-age" does not necessarily denote an actual time period but a metaphorical phase through which a character navigates along their developmental arc.

SEPARATION FROM THE MATERNAL: STEP ONE

Unlike the hero's journey, which starts in the ordinary world, the heroine's journey begins with a separation from the feminine, serving as a reminder of the original maternal offense—eviction from the womb.[2] The heroine experiences a disconnect from the maternal principle in her life, which is often depicted as the mother. The triggering reminder of separation can manifest in several different ways. A young person may fundamentally disapprove of their mother and how she lived her life or the choices she's made. A child may reject their mother's sacrifices on behalf of the family or fail to identify with her passivity. The mother may resent her daughter for having greater opportunity or being ungrateful for her martyrdom. The offspring may internalize this and perceive her mother as vengeful and jealous. A young person may find themselves ensnared in a dichotomy between the yearning for maternal affection and the aspiration to evolve into an autonomous individual. An unevolved mother may stifle a daughter's growth by not allowing her to separate to become her own woman. A son or daughter may also have an ideal relationship with their mother but struggle with feelings of guilt and betrayal at the need to separate and grow into an independent individual.

In story, this stage can be depicted by a separation from the mother, motherland, mother ship, mother tongue, motherhood, mother nature, motherly instincts, or any other maternal figure, symbol, or role model, which may be a deliberate detachment or involuntary. There may be a denial of physical, mental, or spiritual aptitude. At a minimum, the heroine rejects or is abandoned by the feminine. In the fairy tale of "Snow White," Snow White loses her mother, the queen, at birth. As an orphan, she suffers a forced, permanent severing from the maternal.

At the heart of Apuleius's *Metamorphoses* is the tale of Eros and Psyche, which begins with the birth of Psyche into a world that venerates Venus,[3] the mother figure of all Romans due to the fact that her son, Aenius, founded Rome.[4] For the Greeks, Venus is known as Aphrodite, the goddess of love and beauty and the biological mother of Eros (Amor).[5] Psyche, the third daughter of the king and queen of the realm, matures into the most beautiful creature ever beheld, so much so that the temples of Aphrodite fall into ruin as people choose to worship Psyche as the goddess of beauty instead. In anger and envy, Aphrodite sends Eros to make Psyche fall in love with a monster. Psyche endures a betrayal by the paramount mother figure within her realm, provoking a Separation from the Maternal.

In her eponymous fictional autobiography, Jane Eyre begins her personal history as an orphaned child when she lived with her maternal uncle's family as an unwanted connection. Her uncle's wife, Mrs. Reed, makes a point of keeping the unwanted waif at a distance from her own children because "she really must exclude [Jane] from privileges intended only for contented, happy, little children."[6] In lieu of receiving a reception as a dear relative, Jane is bullied and beaten by her cousin. "I was a discord in Gateshead Hall [. . .]. I had nothing in harmony with Mrs. Reed."[7] Jane's disconnect from the maternal principle is evident in the first instance from her mother being dead and in the second from Mrs. Reed's intolerance of her.

Nevertheless, the pivotal occurrence that serves as a reminder of these initial provocative childhood episodes transpires at a subsequent juncture, when Miss Temple leaves Lowood, the crossroad at the end of her hero's journey when there's a clear break in her story after Helen's death. "I now pass a space of eight years almost in silence."[8] Everything changes once her mentor marries a clergyman and moves far away. "She had stood me in the stead of mother, governess, and, latterly, companion."[9] And she notes at length how Miss Temple's absence prompts a sudden dissatisfaction in her life:

> From the day she left I was no longer the same: with her was gone every settled feeling, every association that had made Lowood in some degree a home to me. I had imbibed from her something of her nature and much of her habits: more harmonious thoughts: what seemed better regulated feelings had become the inmates of my mind. I had given in allegiance to duty and order; I was quiet; I believed I was content: to the eyes of others, usually even to my own, I appeared a disciplined and subdued character. [. . .] I walked about the chamber most of the time. I imagined myself only to be regretting my loss, and thinking how to repair it; but when my reflections were concluded, and I looked up and found that the afternoon was gone, and evening far advanced, another discovery dawned on me, namely, that in the interval I had undergone a transforming process; that my mind had put off all it had borrowed of Miss Temple or rather that she had taken with her the serene atmosphere I had been breathing in her vicinity and that now I was left in my natural element, and beginning to feel the stirring of old emotions. It did not seem as if a prop were withdrawn, but rather as if a motive were gone; it was not the power to be tranquil which had failed me, but the reason for tranquility was no more.[10]

As in *Jane Eyre*, *Titanic* is also a fictional autobiography told in retrospect by the aging hundred-year-old Rose DeWitt Bukater Dawson Calvert—indicating that the heroine's journey is completed by a mature adult, despite early childhood beginnings. Entering the picture on a white helicopter named *Sea Stallion*, an animal stereotypically reserved for the white knight hero rescuing a damsel in distress, Rose is deliberately portrayed as the vindicating heroine of her own story. The elder Rose begins the story of young Rose already engaged to Cal, a wealthy heir to a fortune, which was arranged by her mother, a widow and society empress on the brink of destitution without the future prospect of Cal's wealth. Rose is trapped between saving her family from financial ruin and making her own choices, between trying to please her mother and becoming her own person. The *Titanic* ship represents a prison of the choice she's made to follow her mother's example. She struggles with feelings of remorse and guilt at having different ideals that extend beyond the confines of the role as a dutiful daughter. "Outwardly I was everything a well brought up girl should be. Inside, I was screaming."[11] The expedition intended to culminate in a marriage to Cal symbolizes a pending death of herself.

Identifying with the Paternal: Step Two

In step two of the heroine's journey, after the heroine experiences a rejection of the feminine, she overcompensates by identifying with the masculine principles in her life, in Identifying with the Paternal. This occurs unsurprisingly as society reinforces the supremacy of the male perspective. Murdock posits that:

> Male norms have become the social standard for leadership, personal autonomy, and success in this culture, and in comparison women find themselves perceived as lacking competence, intelligence, and power. The girl observes this as she grows up and wants to identify with the glamour, prestige, authority, independence, and money controlled by men. Many high-achieving women are considered *daughters of the father* because they seek the approval and power of that first male model. Somehow mother's approval doesn't matter as much; father defines the feminine, and this affects her sexuality, her ability to relate to men, and her ability to pursue success in the world. Whether a woman feels that it is alright to be ambitious, to have power, to make money, or to have a successful relationship with a man derives from her relationship with her father.[12]

When Identifying with the Paternal, a heroine's objective is to gain power and authority, which may be achieved "either by becoming like men or becoming liked by men."[13] Consequently, the manner in which the heroine identifies with the masculine can assume various expressions. In seeking a father's approval, a heroine may have followed in his footsteps and career, or he may have supported and nurtured her professional growth and social interests in politics, sports, or the arts. A supportive father who encourages a child to take steps towards a definable goal helps a heroine achieve success in a man's world. But they may harbor feelings of guilt over a simultaneous desire to pursue other more feminine interests.

Some heroines fall into this step simply by actively trying to avoid becoming anything like their mothers because of the broken model they provide. Murdock claims, "In cases, where a mother is chronically depressed, ill, or alcoholic, the daughter allies herself with her father, ignoring her mother [. . .]. The father then carries the power not only in the outside world but in her inner world as well."[14] However, not all fathers are positive role models, and some heroines only have access to a negative father-figure. Those heroines overdevelop their inner masculine at the cost of their inner feminine. People who had sabotaging fathers may be caught up in the fruitless endeavor of trying to prove their worth and ultimately struggle to achieve success, despite being well-educated. Such fathers, coupled with absentee mothers, may be suffocating, and those persons may find themselves hopeless and even suicidal.[15]

In terms of story, this stage is depicted by striving to excel, gaining dominance, taking up occupations typically socially or culturally relegated as "manly," which includes masculine jobs, games, disputes, or interests. The heroine may seek out male role models or masculine women or, in turn, be sought out by men for subservience or adoration with which she readily, if not temporarily, submits. In the absence of positive figures, the story's heroine may simply express a wish not to exist, a desperation to be free, or a futile hope of rescue. She could be highly cultured, sublimating all that is earthy, instinctual, native, and natural about her. She may express a fear of vulnerability, display a lack of empathy, gain strength, build Amazonian armor, or develop perfectionism. For Snow White, her father becomes her sole parent and caregiver, and she's absolutely reliant upon him as a child while he rules the land as king. She overidentifies by relating initially to the only paternal influence left in her life.

In Eros and Psyche, despite Psyche's renowned beauty, no one asks to marry her. She's unable to enjoy the ultimate success of being liked by men of her culture—love and marriage. In despair, her father seeks the advice of an ancient oracle god who instructs him to abandon Psyche on a mountaintop for her marriage to a dragon beast. Dressed in funerary costume, her wedding procession is more like a burial procession, filled with sadness and tears. In the final moment, her parents hesitate to comply, but she, nonetheless, fulfills the dictates of the oracle by embracing her fate.[16] In this way, Psyche has done everything to honor her father's will. She lived her life as the most beautiful mortal, which was all her society expected of her despite its failure to fulfill the promise of beauty. She chides her family and friends for weeping over the situation that they caused in their worship of her, a false god, and she boldly proceeds to her imminent demise. In the absence of healthy, supportive parents, she finds no choice but to submit herself to death.

In *Jane Eyre*, Jane taps into masculine elements when she suddenly expresses a desire to be free. "[N]ow I felt that it was not enough: I tired of the routine of eight years in one afternoon. I desired liberty; for liberty I gasped; for liberty I uttered a prayer; it seemed scattered on the wind then faintly blowing."[17] She quickly concludes that she needs a new appointment, placing an advertisement for herself as a governess. Then she appeals to Mr. Brocklehurst for a recommendation letter, identifying with the only male authority of her acquaintance for support. He gives it to her on the condition of Mrs. Reed's approval, which is incidentally granted as a result of her commitment to continue a disassociation from Jane. But then Bessie, Mrs. Reed's servant, follows up by visiting Jane, informing her that she had other paternal interests still at large. Her father's brother had inquired of her whereabouts, searching for her just before he departed on a long voyage as a wine merchant. Finally, when Jane leaves, she "parted at the door of the Brocklehurst Arms," a symbolic image of a fatherly embrace as she leaves.[18]

These incidents of identification mirror an earlier attachment to the masculine at the beginning of her life's account. After Jane's cousin beats her and she labels him a murderer, she's thrown into the unused but preserved room of her late uncle as punishment for her verbal abuse.[19] In the long silence and growing darkness that she's left alone in, she begins to imagine that her uncle would have been kind to her had he lived—an uncle who had extracted a promise from his wife to care for baby Jane as he lay dying in the very bed that loomed large before her.[20] Jane then begins to fantasize that he was so kind that he might even be disturbed enough in his grave at the violation of his last wishes, such that he would revisit "the earth to punish the perjured and avenge the oppressed," as decent dead men were wont to do. "And, I thought, Mr. Reed's spirit, harassed by the wrongs of his sister's child, might quit its abode [. . .] and rise before me in this chamber."[21] Although Jane is consoled by the thought that Mr. Reed's ghost would avenge her, by over-identifying with his power she also scares herself into dead faint.

In *Titanic*, similar to Psyche, Rose fulfills her obligation as the dutiful, beautiful daughter by submitting herself to becoming a trophy wife, as was expected of a young woman of her class. She also shows an awareness of contemporary art, a knowledge of modern psychology, and a familiarity with cigarettes, all practices usually restricted to the male domain at the time. In fact, her mother chides Rose for smoking, a deliberate attempt to further separate herself from her mother, and her fiancé takes the cigarette away from her. He is not particularly charmed by her taste for art, her knowledge of Freud, or her penchant for male indulgences. If Rose had been stifled under her mother, she was being suffocated under the weight of her late father's bad debts and the male figure who refused to let her advance in any way that he did not approve of. She too, like Psyche, sees suicide as her only option. Rose approaches the stern of the ship and contemplates a mortal plunge.

Road of Trials: Step Three

After denying the feminine and over-identifying with the masculine, the heroine arrives at the conclusion that she cannot become her mother or her father—she must become herself. This begins step three in the heroine's journey, what Murdock (and Campbell) calls the "Road of Trials," which starts with a Campbellian Crossing of a Threshold.[22] The heroine leaves the perceived safety of her home to journey through woods, over mountains, and into concrete jungles. She will encounter the "obstacle course that leads to academic degrees, promotions, prestigious titles, marriage, and financial success."[23] Along the way, she meets with tyrants and ogres in the form of her parents, teachers, coworkers, and bosses who will test her strengths and weaknesses. She is internally challenged by self-doubt, self-hate, fear, and paralyzing indecision.[24]

In the process, the heroine must slay the dragons of dependency, inferiority, and/or romantic love. Women of a patriarchal society and feminine men may find themselves discouraged from seeking independence and encouraged to serve others at the expense of serving themselves. The heroine must find the balance between caretaking and independence, because absolute independence where a person delays marriage and a family to establish themselves professionally also does not serve a person's development of self. By the same token, women have a sense of inferiority as a consequence of living in a male-dominated society. The heroine must learn that her wants and demands are not inferior to anyone else's. In doing so, she may have to battle despots and oppressors. Similarly, the heroine may entertain fantasies about romantic love, believing that true happiness is only attained through union with the right partner. As a result, some heroines may be caught in a waiting pattern holding out hope for love while they have to realize that they need to take their own action to bring about wholeness and true happiness.

As an example of this step, Murdock references the myth of Eros and Psyche, compressing the entire myth into the Road of Trials and overlooking its value in relation to the remainder of the journey. She neglects the opportunity to fully utilize mythology as an illustration of her theory, instead focusing more on her personal experience and that of her patients with regards to achieving psychological wholeness. Accordingly, Murdock omits an analysis from the mythological or mythopoeic perspectives.

In story, the heroine finds a job, starts a relationship, goes to school, travels to a new country, enters a labyrinth, wanders alone in the night, searches for her voice, or falls under the spell of illusory love, while experiencing various obstacles along the way. She will be convinced that she could be superwoman without realizing that jealous saboteurs prey upon any possible failure. She may be tempted to manipulate to succeed or she may obsesses over feelings of remorse at letting others down. For example, Snow White's trials begin when her father remarries a stunning woman, a new queen with unsurpassed beauty in the realm and one who jealously guards her glamorous status. Snow White starts a new relationship when she gains a stepmother. Although she was born a fair and pleasing princess, she lives with an evil queen who doesn't wish to see her succeed.

Psyche begins her Road of Trials by crossing a threshold when she leaves her childhood home forever and is left on the top of a mountain. She is saved from the prospect of death by Eros, who has the West Wind whisk her away to a private paradise, where she eventually falls in love with him during his nightly visits. Eros makes her promise not to ever look at him or they will be separated forever, in part because of his refusal to complete the mission from his mother, who commanded him to have Psyche fall in love with a beast. Aphrodite will punish them both for failing her dictates. While Psyche enjoys a paradisiacal abode with Eros, she's only allowed to it if she submits to Eros's rules. This state of connubial bliss only lasts a short time before Psyche's loneliness during the day compels her to want more than conditional love.

Eros begrudgingly allows her to visit and comfort her weeping sisters, who are mourning her loss. No longer as naïve as she once was, Psyche learns that she is pregnant. Like the child growing inside her, she is also maturing and outgrowing the darkness of ignorance. Under these circumstances and aided by the whisperings of her envious sisters, Psyche wonders whether the prophecy was true—that she was married to a monster who would eventually consume her.

In *Jane Eyre*, Jane sets out for her new life as a governess at Thornfield Hall by crossing the threshold of an erstwhile home. As she nears her destination, she says, "I felt we were in a different region to Lowood, more populous, less picturesque; more stirring, less romantic."[25] Jane meets the housekeeper, Mrs. Fairfax, who is relieved to finally have a companion of equal status for the long, cold nights at Thornfield, which is a "fine old hall, rather neglected of late years"[26] Nonetheless, Jane notes, "A very chill and vaultlike air pervaded the stairs and gallery, suggesting cheerless ideas of space and solitude [. . .]."[27] Thus, Jane's new abode appears to be tomb-like. She learns that her employer is enigmatic, suspects that a ghost lives on the third floor, hears the strange cackling attributed to Grace Poole, likens her new home to

Bluebeard's Castle, a reference to a folktale about a murderous husband, and teaches her young orphaned pupil, Adele. Jane meets Mr. Rochester when he falls at her feet, having slipped on ice with his horse. Later, she saves his life when she finds his bed engulfed in flames. Thus, Jane crosses a threshold, enters new relationships, and comes under the spell of romantic love on her Road of Trials.

The similarity to Psyche is noteworthy. Jane lives on a hill in a mausoleum, a vaulted monument feeling at times stifled, buried alive, and, in a sense, left to die in long moments of solitary boredom, despite her employment. "I shall be called discontented. I could not help it: the restlessness was in my nature; it agitated me to pain sometimes."[28] She is taken in by the de facto lord of the manor, a modern-day god of his realm, who likened himself to Apollo and meets with her in the evenings by candlelight. She takes a short vacation to visit with her dying aunt, much to Rochester's disapproval, where she meets up with her two sister-like cousins who despise each other, delaying her return to Thornfield and attending to their needs long after Mrs. Reed's death.

In *Titanic*, Rose crosses a threshold when she decides to climb over the railing of the ship to commit suicide. She takes a moment too long during which Jack sees her and encourages her to reconsider. She listens because there is something about him that calls her back to her senses, and in so doing, she nearly slips off the ship. Jack represents her inner masculine calling her back to life. During the rest of the voyage, Rose befriends Jack, spending increasingly more time with him. He sees the truth of her, that she's a trapped butterfly (A butterfly is another definition for the Greek word psyche).[29] Jack sees that the truth is her soul is entrapped. She tells him, "It's not up to you to save me, Jack."[30] Jack responds by saying, "You're right. Only you can do that,"[31] which shatters the myth of romantic love developing between them in her Road of Trials.

The Boon: Step Four

At the end of the Road of Trials, the heroine believes she succeeded when she arrives at the land of power and independence and is crowned with talismans of achievement as the fourth step. Murdock refers to this as the "illusory boon of success," drawing from Campbell's chapter on "The Ultimate Boon."[32] The heroine has climbed the corporate ladder, is active in the community, has fallen in love, gotten married, had children, bought the dream house, and has in effect become superwoman of the outer world. She enjoys the fruits of her labors, including wealth, expensive property, jewelry, clothes, cars, vacations, accolades, and other experiences. She literally or figuratively reaches a pinnacle, publishes a book, launches a product, outperforms her competitors, or has it all. She has slayed an inner sabotaging voice and, at the same time, faces looming burnout. The heroine must shatter the myth of limitlessness.

In the Grimm fairy tale, Snow White becomes more beautiful than the queen and is crowned the fairest one of all. While this is an achievement that would presumably put her ahead in her father's estimation, let alone the kingdom, this creates a hostile jealousy within the queen who devises a plan to eliminate her competition. Snow White's newfound status is soon to be short-lived.

Stealing a forbidden glimpse of her husband in the darkness, Psyche quickly realizes that she's married to the very god of love.

> But the instant the lamp elucidated the secrets of the bed to which she brought it, she saw the sweetest beast, the gentlest wild thing in the world, Cupid himself, that gorgeous god, at gorgeous rest. [. . .] [A]s she took one peek after another at the exquisite, divine face, her heart was refreshed. She saw the full head of exuberant golden locks, drunk with ambrosia, the neck the color of milk, the purple cheeks with orbs of hair straying around them, gracefully looped up, some hanging in front and some in back. [. . .] The rest of him was as smooth and shiny as a bald head—Venus herself needn't have been ashamed of giving birth to a body like this!"[33]

For someone originally betrothed to a monster, whose marriage bed was her deathbed, discovering her husband a divinity is a boon of success, albeit temporary.

Mr. Rochester proposes to Jane, elevating her to the highest status achievable for someone so "poor, obscure, plain, and little.'[34] He sends for the family jewels that includes a crown so that she could be treated like a "peer's daughter," even though she wasn't.[35] He promises to "attire my Jane in satin and lace, and she shall have roses in her hair; and I will cover the head I love best with a priceless veil,"[36] the outward success and fruit of her unintended labors.

Cal gives Rose his engagement gift to her early, a 56-carat diamond necklace, known as the Heart of the Ocean, to cheer her up right after the scare of her near death. The jewel once belonged to Louis XVI, the last of the absolute monarchs of France. She's overwhelmed to receive it, but Cal reminds her that it's for royalty. "And we are royalty." The necklace was meant to remind Rose of his love but serves as the token of her illusory achievement, having engaged a wealthy heir and been elevated to a regal status. Rose attains another level of success when she learns to trust Jack, and he teaches her how to fly. She moves from nearly drowning by dropping off the stern of the ship to nearly flying off the bow with Jack's help. Where earlier he'd accused her of being a trapped butterfly, now she is free.

Betrayal: Step Five

Once the heroine has been tried and succeeds in the patriarchal world, she begins to feel that there's something missing or out of sync. According to Murdock, "Although they are satisfied with the skills they have mastered, the independence they have achieved, and the influence they now have in their chosen field, there is a feeling of weariness and uncertainty about how to continue."[37] The heroine is not as fulfilled as she thought she would be by pursuing the path she had chosen. She feels betrayed by the false promise of success. Feelings of "spiritual aridity" arise, and the heroine wonders what's next.[38] Step five in the journey is thus marked by a sense of Betrayal, whether the heroine feels betrayed by her self, spouse, children, parents, extended family, friends, coworkers, a community, or society at large. All that she had done in following the dictates of society is not enough for happiness.

In this phase, the heroine then becomes aware of being over-extended. She committed to too many projects and objectives that she realizes do not actually serve her happiness. This is where the heroine needs to learn to say no. Her family and coworkers will begin to think that there's something seriously wrong with her. There comes a time where the heroine has to stop doing things the way that she had been. She might quit a job, refuse an offer, leave a relationship, have a breakdown, lose steam, get sick, or challenge authority. Ultimately, she is repudiating the dominance of the structure of power in her life, which has often been patriarchy for women. Such refutation will not come easily. The people in the heroine's daily life will try to convince her to stay the course that they have laid out for her—the course she might have previously chosen but had lost conviction for. She doesn't realize it yet, but her feminine side is calling to her. The denial of her feminine has come at a cost she no longer wants to pay. She sold her soul for a career, for a relationship, for some *thing* and now she wants it back. She wants a more balanced, authentic life.

Murdock digresses in this chapter to discuss her personal feelings about this stage. "When I first started writing this chapter I began to have dreams about a positive inner masculine figure whom I called the 'kitchen man' because I first encountered him sweeping a kitchen floor."[39] She continues by sharing a passage from her journal in relation to her experience, as further evidence for this stage, which is as problematic as Campbell's authorial fiat for establishing a pattern. Nonetheless, the principle remains subject to investigation and analysis in mythology and story.

For Snow White, the queen commissions her Huntsman to kill the fairest one of all. Snow White is betrayed by her stepmother as well as the Huntsman. She repudiates his authority, pleading with him not to go through with it. The Huntsman relents, expecting instead for the wild beasts of the forest ahead to devour her in any event.

Psyche betrays Eros by violating his rule against seeing him. She pricks herself accidentally with one of his arrows and spills lamp oil on him, which causes Eros to awaken in pain. Because of Psyche's treachery, Eros leaves her, flying away, but she has now found godly love and is not prepared to see it disappear. By the same token, Eros had betrayed Psyche by never revealing his true identity. Had she known she wasn't married to a beast, she might not have feared for her life. Psyche's feelings of isolation and inner voice moved her to challenge the patriarchal order of her little world with Eros. The light she brings to bear on the situation, a light of consciousness, scars and scares Eros off, but for Psyche it's a moment of clarity. According to Gisela Labouvie-Vief who compares Eros and Psyche to the rational and imaginative parts of the mind:

> Jung has suggested that this striving to expose to the "light" what has been hidden by darkness is a major theme of mature development, a process happening around the middle of life. According to his theory, the individual around midlife begins to reevaluate those parts of the self that so far were pushed underground. Having forged a quite successful adaptation to the life according to the norms and rules of one's culture, the individual begins to experience the loss of abandoned and devalued parts of the self. Jung thinks that this sense of loss initiates a search for a new way of being—a way that is no longer dictated by the individual's obedience to the norms and rules of logos, but one that establishes a dialogue between two modes of being and two ways of knowing.[40]

Psyche has now glimpsed the truth and has seen divine love; and she will not know peace until she regains it.

Jane is betrayed at the altar of her wedding when the truth Rochester kept hidden in the attic of Thornfield is revealed. He was already married, and his wife lives on the third floor. Like Eros, Rochester is enraged at the discovery of his secret. Thus, Jane is deceived by Rochester who attempted to become a bigamist by marrying her. Jane also inadvertently betrayed Rochester, when her word of pending nuptials eventually circled back to his brother-in-law, who comes to stop the wedding. Regardless, Rochester does not want Jane to leave. He loves her, and she loves him. That should be sufficient, even if it means she becomes his mistress. But she doesn't accept where she fits in his patriarchal world view. She rejects him and decides to leave Thornfield.

The betrayal that takes place in *Titanic* is not as instantaneous as in Eros and Psyche or in *Jane Eyre*. Slowly, Rose begins to feel the strictures of her patriarchal society as impinging on her personal interests and freedom. After Rose enjoys an evening of dancing in third class with Jack and his friends,

Cal yells at her for not acting like the wife he essentially purchased by coming to him the previous night (presumably to bed). To make his point of dominating power, he explodes with a sweep of the breakfast china off the table. Later, the audience sees Rose's mother, Ruth, vigorously tightening Rose's corset while she reminds her daughter in no uncertain terms about her duty to marry money to bring her family out of her father's debts. Rose exclaims, "It's so unfair." And her mother retorts, "Of course it's unfair! We're women. Our choices are never easy."[41] By "choices," the audience is left to infer the choice between submitting to the patriarchal status quo despite feminine inclinations to the contrary and bucking the patriarchal system to pursue those unexpected nascent feminine desires.

Finally, in a subtle scene where Rose absently listens to her mother drone on with other socialites about the challenges of bridal shopping while she sits quietly to tea, Rose watches another mother and young daughter sitting at a different table having tea while the mother teaches the little girl social etiquette. Rose observes her past and future in that moment. She lived that life, and she can't imagine herself forcing it on a future daughter. In that moment, she makes a choice for matriarchy. She leaves the table in search of Jack, where she finds him at the apex of the bow railing watching the sunset. She joins him and says she feels like she's flying. They share a kiss, and she invites him to her room to draw her as she really is—in the nude because "The last thing I need is another picture of me looking like a china doll."[42] Rose has decided that she's not going to be someone's trophy wife. She leaves the finished drawing for Cal in his safe with a note, effectively betraying their arrangement by terminating their relationship.

Rose continues her escape of patriarchy by running away with Jack, who was her soulmate. They hide away in a brand-new Renault stored in the cargo hold where they consummate their love. After that, Cal reads the note left behind. "Darling, now you can keep us both locked in your safe."[43] With that absolute refutation of the patriarchy in her life, Rose's life is permanently changed, and the *Titanic* hits an iceberg, where nature also conspires to betray them all.

Descending: Step Six

In the next step of the heroine's journey, the heroine enters a state of depression marked by a long period of descent, "characterized as a journey to the underworld, the dark night of the soul, the belly of the whale, the meeting of the dark goddess, or simply as depression," utilizing Campbell's Belly of the Whale and Meeting with the Goddess.[44] Marie-Louise von Franz observes of this period that "From the outside it looks like complete stagnation, but in reality it is a time of initiation and incubation when a deep inner split is cured and inner problems solved. [. . .] The unconscious is experienced as isolation by the heroine, and afterward comes the return into life."[45] Murdock skims through the Mesopotamian myth of Inanna to reflect aspects of the descent as it relates to the psychological experience of surrendering to the unconscious found amongst her patients. However, for mythopoeic purposes, the story of Inanna is rich with symbolism and motif descriptive and illustrative of encounters with the Nether Land, warranting a more considered analysis. As noted, the season of descent is divided in two steps: Step Six, Descending, and Step Seven: Descent Dwelling.

Inanna is the Sumerian queen of heaven and earth, a deity of love and warfare, who is also referred to as Ishtar, a comparable figure of worship by Assyrians, Babylonians, and Akkadians. As the goddess of the great above, she seeks the goddess of the great below, Ereshkigal, who by some accounts is Inanna's sister and twin, to mourn the loss of Gugalanna, Ereshkigal's husband. Inanna abandons seven cities and seven temples dedicated to her veneration as she marches towards Lapis Lazuli Mountain, the gateway to the land of no return known as *Kur*, both an underworld and mountains, representing foreign land or enemy territory.[46] As she passes through seven gates of descent, she is compelled to relinquish one of her divine decrees, the hard won cultural achievements and arts of civilization that she gained from her father, Enki, the lord of wisdom.[47] She removes her crown, lapis lazuli choker, double-stranded beaded necklace, chest plate, gold ring, scepter, and royal robe. The heroine is therefore initiated by removal from a high place or a stepping down, during which she may be stripped of outer accoutrements.

In story as in life, Descending is generally triggered by a sudden change in a person's life, such as loss of a loved one, end of a relationship, or serious health concerns. It can be experienced in terms of a sudden illness, loss in livelihood, a geographical move, the inability to finish a goal, voluntary isolation, a long hike in the woods, or a broken heart. "The journey to the underworld is filled with confusion and grief, alienation and disillusion, rage and despair. A woman may feel naked and exposed, dry and brittle, or raw and turned inside-out."[48] The heroine feels on the brink of tears, sad, and preoccupied while she walks aimless in unfamiliar territory for an untold period of time. The heroine enters a period of grief, rage, loss, denial, and eventually introspection and meditation.

Murdock also associates this stage with the Greek goddess Demeter, as a doorway to secrets of the feminine because she was worshipped for two thousand years as the center of the Eleusinian Mysteries, secretive rituals surrounding the feminine divine. Demeter was the grain goddess who experienced a painful loss when her daughter, Persephone, was kidnapped to the underworld by Hades. The heroine feels like Demeter who hears Persephone's cries and rushes to find her in a frantic search for a damsel in distress, panicking and forgetting to eat, sleep, bathe. Snow White ventures deep into foreign land by escaping into the forest, far from the castle. She gives up all that is cultured and regal for everything rustic and natural. For Snow White, having fled into the forest frightened, she comes across a little house by nightfall, when she is hungry and tired. She nibbles from seven different plates and finds seven little beds, which she tests until she falls asleep on the last one. Her descent is a divesture of all she has known until she collapses of fatigue.

In Eros and Psyche, when Eros flies off in pain, Psyche grabs onto his foot until she loses her grasp and falls to the earth, away from him and their love nest, marking her initial descent. She too has been suddenly stripped of every known comfort. She despairingly throws herself in the nearby river, but the river returns her to the banks where she meets Pan, the shepherd god with the body of a human but face and extremities of a goat. As the namesake of the term *panic*[49] with his own personal history of having lost love in the reeds of a riverbed, Pan takes particular note of the "tottering and uncertain steps of [Psyche], and from [her] deathly pallor, and from [her] continual sighing, and from [her] swimming" and urges her to pray to the god of love for relief.[50] Instead of panicking, he recommends that she supplicate for divine love as the elixir to her earthly woes, or seeking solace from her other half.

Jane's descent begins in the middle of the night when she hears a voice telling her to run away from temptation. "Drearily I wound my way downstairs: I knew what I had to do, and I did it mechanically."[51] Departing from Thornfield, which is situated on a hill, requires a further descent as she wanders aimlessly, feeling like a dead woman walking. "I looked neither to rising sun, nor smiling sky, nor wakening nature. He who is taken out to pass through a fair scene to the scaffold, thinks not of the flowers that smile on his road, but of the block and axe-edge."[52] Like Psyche, she feels guilt over the pain she caused Rochester and her loss, like "a barbed arrow-head in my chest."[53] She expresses self-loathing, grief, loss, and introspection.

> In the midst of my pain of heart, and frantic effort of principle, I abhorred myself [. . .]. As to my own will or conscience, impassioned grief had trampled one and stifled the other. I was weeping wildly as I walked along my solitary way: fast, fast I went, like one delirious. A weakness, beginning inwardly, extending to the limbs, seized me, and I fell: I lay on the ground some minutes, pressing my face to the wet turf.[54]

She rambles through wet fields until she collapses in weakness. She catches a carriage and pays for it with all the money she has, becoming destitute. Inside, she weeps with agony and appeals "to Heaven in prayers" for having been "the instrument of evil to what [she] wholly love[d]."[55] A few days later, Jane ends up at Whitcross, a four-way crossroad in the middle of nowhere, forgetting everything she brought with her in the departing coach. Thus, having arrived at a center of her world, Jane is stripped of all her worldly belongings.

Rose's descent begins voluntarily when she asks the shipbuilder where to find Jack. He gives her clear, but lengthy, instructions that she would find him at the bottom of the ship, passed certain corridors, at the Master-at-Arm's Office. She then fights with the elevator operator, "I'm through being polite, goddamnit."[56] She pushes him into the elevator and demands he take her down to the bottom of the ship. Similar to Inanna's descent, civility is the first accouterment of Rose's society that she gives up at a gate of the descent. In the same instant, she also calls on God for help, albeit to curse those in her way. They descend to a flooded floor, which scares the elevator operator into immediately re-ascending, abandoning Rose to rising water levels and flickering lights as she wades deeper into flickering darkness.

Descent Dwelling: Step Seven

In Descent Dwelling, the heroine faces off with her mirror, a twin, a dark mother, or judging force. The Descent Dwelling draws from Campbell's Crossing of the First Threshold, the Belly of the Whale, Meeting with the Goddess, and Woman as Temptress. But the marked difference, in this case, centers around the heroine who hasn't arrived to conquer her worst enemy, intent on swiping a treasure to return from the same entrance. Instead, she seeks a new way out, a new way of being. This represents unknown and, for all intents and purposes, illogical territory. She can't rely on old skills of goal making and logical thinking—skills that brought her to this point to begin with—to guide her through the yawning canyon suddenly before her. Without the capacity to reason out of the problem, she understands that there are no obvious answers. The heroine is naked, walking in silence among the dead, upon a moist, cold earth, feeling isolated or abandoned. During this phase, a person tries to reclaim the lost parts of themselves that were previously blocked off as irrelevant or worthless—especially feminine aspects such as instinct, intuition, faith, and nonlinear thought. The heroine's ultimate task is to learn to harness the powers of her unconscious and merge those with her conscious powers. According to von Franz, "There are such situations where one has to wait, and noninterference is the healing factor."[57]

In story, Descent Dwelling appears when the heroine hits rock bottom, which can be characterized by depression, sadness, fruitlessness, rage, anger, breakdown, rawness, nakedness, denial, loss, and/or an overwhelming sense of pending doom or death. Often she meets with her mirror, a twin version of herself, where she finally notices all of her neglected aspects. What the heroine has achieved in the world counterbalances against the sacrificed missing parts. In a moment of recognition of the feminine principle in one's self, she becomes introspective and meditative. She must abandon habits and skills that served as strengths in her old world of accomplishments and express more instinct, compassion, wisdom, healing, and spirituality.

In the myth of Inanna, Inanna appears finally before Ereshkigal completely stripped and humbled. The seven judges of the Anunnaki pronounce her guilty, "the[ir] word tortures [her] spirit,"[58] and her corpse is hung like raw meat. Ereshkigal represents Inanna's shadow as her twin sister or mirror image—reflecting all the internal parts of Inanna that is unloved, abandoned, instinctual, raging, greedy, desperate, and lonely. According to Sumerian mythology expert, Samuel Noel Kramer, "All that Inanna had achieved on earth weighs against her when she meets the woman at whose expense Inanna's glories had been attained."[59] But Inanna left behind Ninshubur, her assistant and servant of their holy shrine, with instructions to help her if she doesn't return from the descent. Inanna had to allow herself to be, trusting in the existence of other, feminine processes, to resolve her suspended and paralytic state. According to Diane Wolkstein and Samuel Noah Kramer, "Inanna's *sukkal* Ninshubur [. . .] seems to represent the inner spiritual resources of Inanna."[60] The term *sukkal* encompasses more than the subservience of an assistant. A *sukkal* has strengths greater than his or her master and can have access to "heavenly, numinous powers."[61] In effect, Ninshubur is Inanna's guardian angel. When she realizes that Inanna needs rescuing, she first appeals to Inanna's father and paternal grandparent. Failing to appreciate the logic of Inanna's deliberate descent, they both refuse to help. Ninshubur than entreats Inanna's maternal grandfather, Enki. He fashions two "artistic and empathetic" androgynous creatures from the dirt of his fingernails, Kurgarra, armed with the food of life, and Galatur, armed with the water of life, to mourn with Ereshkigal, thereby soothing her loneliness, grief, and anger.[62] Kurgarra and Galatur moan and sigh with her as she gives birth. Relieved by their support, Ereshkigal offers them a gift, and they choose Inanna's corpse, which they sprinkle with the water and food of life. Therefore, in the expression of art and empathy, a heroine may find her way out of the underworld, rebirthed.

For Snow White, like the judges of the Anunnaki, seven, dark, master underground diggers return to their home to find that their chair, plate, loaf, porridge, fork, knife, and cup have been touched. They stand by Snow White's bed, judging her and concluding that she is just a child, and presumably as innocent as one. They decide to allow her to continue to sleep.

Psyche wanders upon Demeter's temple where she discovers it in disarray and sets upon putting worshipful offerings of wheat to order, while praying for help, an expression of introspection and meditation. She weeps at Demeter's feet as her hair falls to the earth, begging for a place of rest.

But Demeter tells her to leave immediately and to be grateful "that you are not my prisoner."[63] Deeply disappointed, Psyche does not realize that to be imprisoned in Demeter's world of sadness would end Psyche's journey and growth. Psyche proceeds to another temple and prays to Hera, Demeter's sister and goddess of marriage, for guidance. But Hera cannot help her against Aphrodite, her daughter-in-law, and the laws which forbade aiding a runaway slave. Aphrodite had even put out an award for Psyche's capture, seven kisses and one tongue thrust. Psyche realizes that in order to find Eros, she must confront Aphrodite, which presents a conundrum. In order to find her love, she must submit herself to the wrath of, and certain death by, Aphrodite, who is still upset with Psyche for not marrying the monster as planned.

Psyche then meets with Habit, her mother-in-law's servant, who drags her before Aphrodite—the metaphorical twin, as they are both venerated, incomparable beauties, both vying for Eros's attention. Aphrodite summons her handmaidens, Care and Sorrow, similar to Kurgarra and Galatur, who further torment Psyche in her anxious condition over Eros.[64] After that, Aphrodite slashes Psyche's clothes and beats her into an ugly state. Only then does Aphrodite relent and consider Psyche properly prepared to earn the goddess's favor by completing four tasks of "diligent drudgery."[65]

In *Jane Eyre*, not knowing where to go, Jane claims, "I have no relative but the Universal Mother: Nature. I will seek her breast and ask repose,"[66] a reference to meeting with the dark mother. Jane heads for the heath, burrows into a hollow, and tucks under a crag. Upon waking, she disappointedly wishes that she had not, "that my Maker thought that night good to require my soul of me while I slept; and that this weary frame, absolved of death from further conflict with fate, had not but to decay quietly [. . .]."[67] She walks for a long time, exhausted, and comes upon a village. She approaches one shop, hoping for food but asking for work. The woman there says that she cannot help. Like Psyche, appealing from goddess to goddess, Jane seeks out other women or possible places of work. She fails to pawn her worn out gloves and handkerchief and finally humbles herself to beg desperately for food. Jane wanders off into the night and sleeps fitfully on wet earth, only to repeat the day she'd had before. She prays, "Oh, Providence! sustain me a little longer! Aid direct me!"[68] She spends some time Descent Dwelling until, at last, a light glows on a twilit horizon.

In *Titanic*, Rose's Descent Dwelling begins when she discovers Jack handcuffed to a water pipe in the Master-at-Arm's Office with the water rising around him. Instead of herself, like Inanna, she finds her better half pegged to a wall. She apologizes to him for not believing immediately in his innocence because "I just realized I already knew," that he didn't commit the crime.[69] Rose has begun to rely on her instinct to guide her.

Rose's next task is to unlock Jack's handcuffs. Failing to find a key, she runs for aid up to the next level. She calls for help when a man with "eyes crazed" runs passed her, ignoring her. Cameron describes this moment "like a bad dream. The hull gongs with terrifying sounds."[70] The lights flicker off, leaving abject darkness during which she starts to hyperventilate. Cameron explains, "That one moment of blackness was the most terrifying of her life."[71] The lights return and a steward appears rushing with lifejackets. She thinks he can help, but he just wants to forcibly drag her back up to safety. She digs her heels, shouts at him, and punches him in the face to get him to release her. He leaves, and she closes her eyes in a moment in despair. When she opens them again, she sees a glass case with a fire-axe. She breaks the case open and takes the axe. Again, she calls on God, saying "Oh my God," as water rises.[72]

Jack insists she swing for his cuffs. "I trust you."[73] They both close their eyes, using blind faith, as she breaks the chain. With a flooded exit, they must search for another way out. Finally, they reach the upper level and search for empty lifeboats because the entire ship is still taking them down for a permanent descent into the Atlantic Ocean. The Descent Dwelling is fraught with a long struggle to escape and pending doom.

Yearning to Reconnect: Step Eight

As a result of the descent, wherein a woman realizes that she needs to find the lost pieces of her severed self, according to Murdock, she develops a sudden "urgent yearning to connect with the feminine," with elements of Campbell's Meeting with the Goddess and Woman as Temptress.[74] The most straightforward manner in which a woman can reconnect with the feminine is to reconnect with her body, now purified from cultural irreverence and divested of any sense of inferiority. "Through conscious nutrition, exercise, bathing, rest-taking, healing, lovemaking, birthing, and dying, [the heroine] reminds us of the sanctity of the feminine for all of us."[75] This epitomizes the time a person engages with their true feelings.

This stage, however, is not without grief. A heroine may feel "rage about the time sacrificed, confusion about the betrayals left unaddressed, sadness for having abandoned herself for so long, and helplessness about taking the next step."[76] As such, a heroine needs to be allowed to grieve in the time and fashion that suits her. In the process of reconnecting, the heroine also becomes more creative. As Murdock explains, "she yearns for the mist, green juicy aspects of the creative feminine [. . .]. This sense of renewal may occur in the garden, in the kitchen, in decorating the home, in relationship, in weaving, writing, or dance. Her sense of aesthetics and sensuality come alive as she is refreshed by color, smell, taste, touch, and sound."[77] As a result, the heroine also learns to let things happen "in the natural cycle of things" and to trust that "the mystery of manifestation is one of the deep teachings of the feminine journey."[78] Another sacred task of the feminine is learning how to *be* and not *do*. "Being requires accepting oneself, staying within oneself, and not *doing* to prove oneself."

In story, this stage appears when a character yearns for connection, which can occur with people, nature, or aspects of one's physical or metaphysical self. At the same time, the heroine may demand an accounting of past betrayals or feel powerless about her future. For Snow White, she reconnects with the feminine by taking on the house chores which includes cleaning, cooking, bed making, washing, sewing, and knitting, which she commits to with all her heart.

Psyche reconnects with the feminine by slowly fulfilling Aphrodite's tasks, which require her to submit to the secrets of nature. In the first task, Psyche must sort through a hill of mixed beans. Psyche freezes at the thought of so daunting a task. In the meantime, ants, what Apuleius refers to as the "children of Earth the all-mother," take pity on her and sort the pile for Psyche.[79] Essentially, Psyche's first lesson requires her to learn to trust in the "mystery of manifestation," where earth's army help Psyche tend to yonic elements such as beans.[80] In discussing the meaning of the ants establishing order out of chaos, Marie-Louise von Franz argues that "[t]his is something which Christian theologians would call faith."[81] According to Erich Neumann, "An unconscious spiritual principle is already at work within Psyche. It works for her and by putting order into matter makes it serviceable to her."[82]

Psyche's second task is to collect golden wool from rams on the riverbank. Again she despairs, and again she is aided by nature, when the "divinely inspired" green reed speaks to her about the safest way to gather wool, by waiting until midday when the sharp-horned sheep were asleep.[83] Thus Psyche must rely on divine wisdom to steal fleece from angry sheep, which represent the destructive masculine aspects of the psyche as well as solar energy.[84] Von Franz argues that "[t]here is an instinct of truth in the human psyche which, in the long run, cannot be suppressed. We can pretend not to hear it, but it remains in the unconscious."[85]

Psyche's third task requires her to gather an urn of water from the icy waterfalls of the River Styx, near the crag of a steep mountain surrounded by snakes and dragons and guarded by the goddess Styx. While Psyche hesitates at the daunting task, an eagle flies to her aid and fills the vessel for her. According to von Franz, "The Styx symbolizes the frightening aspect of the mother archetype and in a certain sense also of the collective unconscious."[86] The River Styx represents the creative and uncontainable energy of the unconscious. "Psyche then, as feminine vessel, is ordered to contain the stream, to give form and rest to what is formless and flowing; as vessel of individuation, as mandala-urn, she is ordered to mark off a configured unity from the flowing energy of life, to give form to life."[87] Psyche is again aided by divine intervention when Zeus sends his eagle to help her.

Charlotte Brontë also sends Jane Eyre on a path to reunite with the feminine principle when Jane stares into Diana and Mary's window, avidly watching them, wishing to be among them. "I had been so intent on watching them, their appearance and conversation had excited in me so keen an interest, I had half-forgotten my own wretched position [. . .]."[88] She knocks on their door, hoping to appeal to their kindness, but the housekeeper thwarts her. St. John, Diana and Mary's brother, saves her by inviting her inside, offering her shelter and respite.

> Somehow, now that I had once crossed the threshold of this house, and once was brought face to face with its owners, I felt no longer outcast, vagrant, and disowned by the wide world. I dared to put off the mendicant to resume my natural manner and character. I began once more to know myself; and when Mr. St. John demanded an account which at present I was far too weak to render I said after.[89]

She rests for three days, regaining strength and health lost in the previous untold days of starvation and deprivation. Diana and Mary whisper compassionate thoughts about her. In yearning to reconnect, Jane heals her body and nourishes her soul in the company of empathetic women.

In the *Titanic*, Jack, joined by Cal, attempts to convince Rose to join a lifeboat, which is only accepting women. Although she doesn't want to leave Jack, the boat full of women, which includes her mother and Mrs. Brown, lures her to stay connected to the feminine. As the vessel lowers, she realizes that she is leaving a part of herself behind, and it's painful. According to Cameron, "A rocket bursts above in slow-motion, outlining Jack in a halo of light . . . Rose's hair blowing in slow motion as she gazes up at him, descending away from him . . . she sees his hand trembling, the tears at the corners of his eyes, and cannot believe the unbearable pain she is feeling."[90] Rose sees Jack for the divine love that he is and in that moment makes a decision to jump off the lifeboat and rejoin him. Rose shows courage and self-sacrifice to be with her love. She yearns to reconnect with him.

Healing the Mother/Child Divide: Step Nine

Finally, after reconnecting with the feminine elements, a heroine must heal the Mother/Child split, which represents a deep divide in one's feminine nature. In some sense, this step relates to healing the separation between mother and child that occurred at birth—the abrupt awakening experienced upon being expelled from the womb. Murdock specifically references this as the mother/daughter split, unnecessarily genderizing an experience that befalls every person born. Curing this split becomes especially difficult for orphans, including emotional orphans—those people who experienced a lack of mothering as children. Early on, before a child grows and learns, the mother represents the totality of the Self. Healing the disconnect allows a heroine to begin to understand how to return to one's Self.

Thus, in this stage, the heroine may seek reunion with the mother, grand-mother, motherhood, motherland, or home. In the absence of that, the heroine will need to forgive and let go. In regard to story-crafting, this may be depicted in terms of cathartic conversations with a mother, dreams of a grandmother, or interacting with goddess myths or figures. A heroine may find healing in "divine ordinariness,"[91] a phase where a heroine might return to a craft or resume a project, decide to organize, finish a pile of ironing, play endless hours of a mindless game, engage in needlework, or do something similarly mundane and intellectually under-stimulating in the subconscious pursuit of divine ordinariness. The heroine may heal the mother/child divide by finding or connecting with community, a space where her voice is heard and welcome, a place of protection. In addition, a stepmother figure may be reproached or redeemed.

In "Snow White," the stepmother discovers that Snow White still lives and decides to murder her. Disguised as a peddler, an old woman, and a peasant, the queen makes three separate attempts on Snow White's life, by bodice lace, poisoned comb, and a toxic apple, where she finally succeeds with the latter. The dwarfs discover Snow White's lifeless body. Unable to revive her, they lay her on a bier to mourn her for three days. Unwilling to bury an unde-caying body, they place her in a glass coffin on a mountain that they guard as an owl (associated with the goddess of wisdom, Athena), raven (associated with the Athena's half-brother Apollo, god of truth), and then a dove (associ-ated with Aphrodite) mourn her. These three symbols reflect the development of Snow White's unconscious, assimilating wisdom and truth, and awaiting by love. Snow White heals the rift created by her stepmother in the company of supporters who love and mourn her.

Aphrodite's first three tasks set up Psyche's final task, where she must travel to the underworld to retrieve a beauty balm from Persephone. Psyche must meet with the mother of the underworld by returning to the World Womb. The assignment scares Psyche by the depth of challenge, and she would rather fling herself off the nearest highest tower. When she attempts it, the tower speaks to her and convinces her not to throw away her life. Instead, it provides necessary instructions of how to perform the journey and return unscathed, with emphasis on not opening the beauty box she carries. Her first step is to enter the underworld through the Vent of Dis, a yonic reference to the entrance of the World Womb, consciously returning to the earth mother. Psyche carries a barley cake in each hand and two coins in her mouth, a sign to keep busy and stay silent while tempted to stray from the course to help the unhelpable, such as saving a drowned dead man. Psyche should only pay for passage across the river of death, feed the mongrels guarding Persephone's castle, and consume coarse bread at Persephone's table, a symbol of humility. At last, Psyche returns safely to earth with divine beauty in hand, which she chooses to anoint herself with, going against all admonitions to the contrary. Over-awed by its contents, Psyche loses consciousness. Psyche's journey into the underworld illustrates rebirth, beginning with the phallic tower from where she begins her journey, continuing with the seeds of life she carries with her for safe passage, and eating from the food of the soul at the heart of the underworld. She finally heals the mother/child divide when she shares in her mother-in-law's salve.

Diana and Mary welcome Jane into their home, where she finds kinship. Additionally, on mythological and Biblical levels respectively, Jane is watched over by the moon and nature goddess, Diana, and the mother figure of Christianity, Mary. Jane then finds community as a teacher, when she takes over the village school and becomes engaged in the mundane task of teaching "coarsely-clad little peasants" to read and write.[92] She later confesses, "Much enjoyment I do not expect in the life opening before me: yet it will, doubtless, if I regulate my mind, and exert my powers as I ought, yield me enough to live on from day to day."[93] However, in her free time, Jane finds creative expression in her art, which her peers praise. Eventually, "I felt I became a favourite in the neighborhood."[94]

Through St. John, Jane learns not only that she is related to them, as long-lost maternal cousins, but that she is also heir to 20,000 pounds, which was the subject of dispute between St. John's father and their uncle. Out of sympathy for their loss, Jane decides to split the inheritance four ways, thereby healing a long-suffering maternal divide.

When the *Titanic* takes a final deep plunge into the ocean, abducting its occupants, Rose survives with the sacrifices Jack makes, releasing her only when she promises not to give up on life, not unlike Inanna's *sukkal* who brings Inanna back to earth. Rose is rescued by the steamship, *Carpathia*, which represents the Great Mother, a symbol of a sheltering place of transformation. Rose climbs on board ascending out of the threat of the underworld that claimed Jack. She will not be able to heal the split from her own mother because that, and all connection to her mother's lifestyle, was necessarily severed when Rose decided to pursue Jack and leave her mom behind in the lifeboat. However, once Rose sees the Statue of Liberty figuratively welcoming her home, she is embraced by her motherland. She has a full life—off screen—where she becomes an actress, learns to fly, travels to Africa, marries, has children, become a grandmother, keeps a menagerie of pets, collects ethnic art, and makes pottery. Thus, Rose also heals the maternal divide by becoming an artist, mother, grandmother, and animal caretaker.

Man with a Heart: Step Ten

Once a person on a heroine's journey has reconnected and internalized the feminine principle, it's time to reunite with the masculine principle to bring psychic balance. For Murdock, this means allowing the creative feminine to heal the inner tyrant, relying on the Grail legend to illustrate her point.[95] The grail is the feminine principle that has the power to heal the Fisher King but doesn't because the Fisher King lost his connection to it by an act of disrespect committed long ago against the feminine. The grail can only be used when Parsifal, "the innocent" and descendant of the king, remembers to ask the king "what ails thee?" Parsifal represents the younger self of the king before he was wounded. When the king sees Parsifal and is asked "what ails thee?" the king recognizes himself in Parsifal, like a mirror. In that moment, the king steps outside of himself, seeing himself through his own younger, undamaged eyes. Only then does the king become aware of himself and what ails him, of his anima and what ails it—finally making conscious what was unconscious. The king needs his anima to come forth and help him see. Becoming aware of and remaining present to the wounded masculine triggers the healing response of the inner feminine. Parsifal functions as the inner feminine although in story he's gendered male.

Signs of an unruly inner masculine are exhibited through character drives for perfection, control, domination, or unattainable satisfaction. "When [the masculine archetypal force] becomes unbalanced and unrelated to life it becomes combative, critical, and destructive. This unrelated archetypal masculine can be cold and inhuman; it does not take into account our human limitations. Its machismo tells us to forge ahead no matter what the cost."[96] Creating balance "requires a conscious sacrifice of mindless attachments to ego power, financial gain, and hypnotic, passive living. It takes courage, compassion, humility, and time."[97] In a word, it takes love—love will harmonize the masculine and feminine.

Ultimately, the heroine attempts to connect with a positive inner masculine, the Man with a Heart, which derives from Campbell's chapter on Atonement with the Father. For Murdock, "He will support her with compassion and strength to heal her tired ego and reclaim her deep feminine wisdom. For this positive man with heart to emerge she needs to honor her feminine nature."[98] In the story of Inanna, Inanna returns to find that the former shepherd, current king and her husband, Dumuzi, has not only become comfortable on the throne, he has risen in authority and forgotten about her while she went through an ordeal in the underworld.[99] Angered by his lack of concern and needing to fulfill the promise to Ereshkigal of sending a substitute in her place, Inanna damns Dumuzi to the underworld. Only then will Inanna and Dumuzi truly be equals. But Dumuzi is unruly and does not take this lightly. In a fit of terror, he runs off on his own adventure before succumbing to a transformative journey that leads inescapably to the underworld. Once there, Inanna and Dumuzi's twin sister weep for him. With the help of Dumuzi's sister and a fly, Inanna rescues Dumuzi from his fate, restoring him by her side.

In story, this step may be depicted as either subduing a tyrannical force or finding a kind person with masculine qualities, which may be reflected in the heroine falling in love or having connected with a good man, reconnecting with a paternal figure, or healing through love. In "Snow White," the prince famously rescues Snow White, pleading to the dwarfs to release her into his care because he could not live without her. Upon his promise to honor and cherish her, the dwarfs take pity on him and relinquish her casket. On the way down from the mountain of her tomb, her body is jostled, and a piece of the poisoned apple dislodges from her throat. She awakens to find that she had been saved by the man with her heart. In the famed Disney version, Walter Disney collapses these acts into a single kiss.

Psyche falls into a deep Snow-White sleep. Eros, having finally recovered from his injuries, misses his beloved and flies to her, finding her unconscious. Pricking her painlessly with one of his arrows, he awakens her and encourages her to finish her final task for Aphrodite while he takes up Psyche's cause with Zeus. Where he was previously portrayed as a boy, playing childish antics, Eros becomes the man with the heart who pleads Psyche's case for divinity to Zeus and succeeds. Psyche is not proactive in this stage. She doesn't directly bring Eros back to her. In a sense, for Psyche to call upon Eros, who represents her inner man, she must activate his heroism. When Psyche dies to her old self, her true inner man (her animus) is ready to embrace and comfort her, giving her the fortitude to awaken to her new self. A person's final transformation comes through divine intervention, a gift of supernatural beings. As N.J. Girardot argues, "Ultimately, initiation is the fortuitous work of the gods (however they are disguised). Heroes and heroines in fairy tales, more so than in epic or saga, do not ordinarily succeed because they act, but because they allow themselves to be acted upon—helped, protected, saved, or transformed—by the magic of the fairy world."[100] In essence, the function of the heroine is not only to love but to *be* loved.

Similarly, Jane finds herself embattling the ruthless and cold St. John for her soul. He wants her to join him in God's work in India as his wife, while she is willing to go but unwilling to give her heart to someone who does not want it. Jane describes St. John as having an "austere and despotic nature" and "cool, inflexible judgement," which is similar to Murdock's description of the heroine's inner tyrant.[101] She must not allow him to rule her. But at the climax of their discussion on the matter he almost persuades her when he softens and shows kindness. St. John is also described as handsome, which makes him, along with his icy nature, analogous to a cold beauty balm.[102] As Jane finds herself yielding, her heart slows and her mind clouds up, indicating an imminent faint:

> I stood motionless under my hierophant's touch. My refusals were forgot-ten—my fears overcome—my wrestlings paralyzed. The Impossible—that is, my marriage with St. John—was fast becoming the Possible. All was changing utterly with a sudden sweep. Religion called—Angels beckoned—God com-manded—life rolled together like a scroll—death's gates opening, showed eter-nity beyond: it seemed that for safety and bliss there, all here might be sacrificed in a second. The dim room was full of visions.[103]

For a brief moment, Jane considers taking the shortcut by taking from the beauty balm. And for that moment, St. John practically lulls her into a Stygian sleep. It's only the sound of Rochester's voice calling her name that "acted on my senses as if their utmost activity hitherto had been but torpor, from which they were now summoned and forced to wake."[104] Like Eros, Rochester awakens his beloved from a potential death. "I broke from St. John, who had followed, and would have detained me. It was *my* time to assume ascendancy. *My* powers were in play and in force."[105] She leaves St. John then and sets out to find Rochester, the man with her heart.

For Jane, fighting the inner tyrant and healing the wounded masculine are depicted separately. Once she is free of the tyrant, she describes herself "like the messenger-pigeon flying home" and finds Mr. Rochester recuperating from his own near-death experience, similar to Dumuzi's descent.[106] Rochester gropes around in the darkness, having been blinded by the fire that burnt down Thornfield and claimed his wife. Jane brings him a glass of water (grail) and candles (light) because "he always has candles brought in at dark, though he is blind."[107] Rochester is conscious and present to his flaws. Jane tends to Rochester's wellbeing, healing him slowly and promising that "you shall not be left desolate so long as I live."[108]

In the *Titanic*, Rose's inner masculine (Jack) is wounded (mortally) when she releases him, plunging him into the bottom of the sea. The healing of her inner masculine begins when she boards the white *Sea Stallion* helicopter and is flown to the *Keldysh*, a research vessel, named after a Russian hero of noble descent and commissioned with searching for the Heart of the Ocean, a large blue diamond believed to be lost in the *Titanic*.[109] The treasure hunter search-ing for the jewel is Brock Lovett, who doesn't believe Rose had anything to do with the *Titanic* since her name doesn't appear on the passenger manifest.

Rose asks to see the artwork that Brock recovered of Jack's drawing of her, with the Heart of the Ocean around her neck. Here she sees her true self, the way Jack saw her. Eventually, she tells everyone the story of how she came to be in that drawing.

In sharing her account of what happened, she converts Lovett by the end of the movie from a money-hungry skeptic to a believer in greater things, like love. His conversion is symbolic of her making peace with the inner tyrant and finding a man with a heart. Afterwards, she steals away quietly in the middle of the night and throws the blue diamond overboard, finally laying to rest what never should have been hers to begin with—a necklace with a long history of disrepute. She had meant to return the ugly necklace to her fiancé, but he slipped it back into the jacket that she escaped in. Rose's act of burying the diamond at sea serves a dual purpose: it symbolizes her taming of the tyrants who previously owned the jewel, and it signifies a final severance from all connections to the oppressors of her past life.

Union: Step Eleven

Murdock fuses together the final three steps of Man with a Heart, Union, and Bliss into a single stage. However, for mythopoeic reasons each event warrants its own step—the final two necessitating separate discussions, although often they occur in very quick succession. In the eleventh step of the heroine's journey, a union occurs, a sacred marriage referred to as *hieros gamos*, which is derived from the mythic marriage of the Greek deities, Zeus and Hera.[110] In a psychological sense, the Ego and the Self unite, consciousness merges with the unconscious. Union derives in part from Campbell's Master of Two Worlds and Apotheosis. The feminine and masculine aspects of one's nature are completely incorporated and accepted together—a syzygy.[111] In a mystical sense, "the soul of the body is made spiritual and the spiritual is embodied."[112] Transcendence is depicted through a magical flight, reverting to Campbell's Magic Flight, an expression of autonomy.

In story, Union can be depicted as an actual wedding ceremony, partnership, family reunion, an embrace, a heavenly ascent, or a coming together of two people on a new plane of understanding—a consummation of sorts. The heroine has transcended the earthly toils of her life that have previously held her back, the proof of which comes in the next stage (with a birth symbol). But in this moment, the heroine is at perfect peace with herself and the world around her for she has reconnected with that part of herself that is eternal. In spiritual terms, she has rediscovered her eternal connection to God. In "Snow White," the prince confesses his love and marries Snow White.

Eros flies to the heavens to plead for Psyche's case before Zeus, which is granted. At their wedding, Zeus proclaims that "[Eros] shall never leave your arms, but your marriage shall endure forever."[113] In marrying Eros, Psyche is welcomed into the kingdom of heaven, where "she attains illumination and deification."[114] The union is symbolic of transcendence. "[T]he symbol of the *hieros gamos* is no longer experienced concretely on the bodily level, but on a higher, psychic one as the union of God with his congregation (the *corpus mysticum*). To put it in modern psychological language, this projection of the *hieros gamos* signifies the conjunction of conscious and unconscious, the transcendent function characteristic of the individuation process," according to Jung—a sacred marriage for the divine syzygy.[115] The bond between Eros and Psyche is everlasting.

In *Jane Eyre*, Jane marries Rochester. By her own account, they live happily ever after. "I know what it is to live entirely for and with what I love best on earth. I hold myself supremely blest—blest beyond what language can express; because I am my husband's life as fully as he is mine."[116] Their union transcends rational measures of language and description, especially when she declares, "No woman was ever nearer to her mate than I am: ever more absolutely bone of his bone and flesh of his flesh."[117] Consequently, "we are ever together," linked for eternity on earth.

In *Titanic*, the final two steps of the heroine's journey are fused together practically in one scene. Rose falls asleep, possibly forever, and finds herself flying towards her beloved in heaven, ascending the grand staircase of the first-class section in a restored *Titanic*, surrounded by her friends and new family as if arriving to the altar of her wedding, not unlike the way in which Psyche ascends to heaven to wed Eros before Zeus and all the other mythic gods. Jack is waiting with his back to the staircase, admiring the stopped clock of Honor and Glory Crowning Time, by Charles Wilson, as if time stood still until that moment. When he realizes that Rose has arrived, he turns around to receive her. They embrace and share a kiss, the implication being, this is their heavenly union, with all the angelic souls who died on the *Titanic* standing witness and applauding. For Jung, the clock is a mandala that simultaneously represents the perpetual movement, i.e., forever, and a squaring of the circle, which in psycho-religious terms means "the union of the soul with God."[118] The clock is the symbol of the sublime coupling of Jack and Rose. In an interview about the final scene of the movie, James Cameron says, "When you love someone you cannot imagine an end to that love [. . .] that you won't be reunited. I think this is a basic psychological need that drives spirituality. And even though there are many people who *don't* believe this, they would *like* to. Such a universal yearning is a powerful force to tap into."[119]

Bliss: Step Twelve

The final step in the heroine's journey is proof of the divine union by the creation of happiness, bliss, ecstasy, joy, pleasure, or rapture. As Murdock contends, "The sacred marriage conjoins the opposites, giving birth to ecstatic wholeness."[120] In story, this may be seen by the actual birth of a child, or it may be the discovery of a precious stone, gold, salt, elixir, or the philosopher's stone. The heroine may finally complete a project, finish a book, fulfill a longstanding duty, begin a new venture, pass the baton, or deliver the mantle of authority. Ultimately, a balanced feminine and masculine psyche of a person lives in a state of bliss; the heroine has become the master of two worlds, the conscious and unconscious. Here, Campbell's last two steps are restored and merged. In "Snow White," there's a passing of the mantle of authority when the magic mirror proclaims the new young queen as a thousand times fairer than before, having surpassed her stepmother as the fairest one of all times.

Psyche gives birth to a baby girl, named Bliss. Because Psyche has been deified, her child is considered heavenly. As indicated by Neumann, "This child is the mystical joy which among all peoples is described as the fruit of the highest mystical union."[121] The experience of bliss is proof of the mystical union of the Ego and Self.

Similarly, Jane also has a child with Mr. Rochester, which Jane only briefly mentions at the end as being a boy. She remarks that when Rochester sees his son with brilliant and black eyes, a union of both darkness and light, "on that occasion, [Mr. Rochester] again, with a full heart, acknowledged that God had tempered judgment with mercy."[122] Jane's child is therefore proof of their wedded bliss, in heroine terms.

Finally, in *Titanic*, the proof of bliss is inferred from the final shot, with Jack and Rose locked in an embrace and the audience gazing into the skylight through the dome above them. Even though Rose descends in her Stygian sleep, she ascends to heavenly heights at the end. Their eternal bliss is confirmed by the film's final score, "My Heart Will Go On" sung by Celine Dion.[123] In it, Dion reiterates the love story, confirming that love is forever, regardless of time or space. Speaking on behalf of Rose, she says, "You're here, there's nothing I fear. And I know that my heart will go on."[124] Rose and Jack's eternal love is immortalized in song, which is the inferred proof of their bliss.

Murdock's phenomenological, hermeneutical, and at times ethnographic explication of the heroine's journey as derived from Campbell and experienced by herself and women she's met in practice reveals a pattern that can also be seen in mythology and story. The twelve steps of the heroine's journey, taken and reordered from Campbell's original seventeen, are confirmed by Eros and Psyche, *Jane Eyre*, and *Titanic*. The hero and heroine's journeys together as a rebooted monomyth reveal that Campbell's mythological reduction with the appropriate adjustments in accordance with principles of individuation continues to speak to the journey of a lived life, from coming of age to coming of middle age.

NOTES

1. Murdock, *The Heroine's Journey: Woman's Guide to Wholeness.*
2. Murdock, *The Heroine's Journey: Woman's Guide to Wholeness*, 17.
3. Neumann, *Amor*, 3.
4. Hamilton, *Mythology*, 320.
5. Hamilton, *Mythology*, 33. Eros is also known as Cupid in Roman mythology.
6. Brontë, *Jane Eyre*, 1.
7. Brontë, *Jane Eyre*, 11.
8. Brontë, *Jane Eyre*, 96.
9. Brontë, *Jane Eyre*, 96.
10. Brontë, *Jane Eyre*, 97–98.
11. Cameron, *Screenplay*, 34.
12. Murdock, *The Heroine's Journey: Woman's Guide to Wholeness*, 29.
13. Murdock, *The Heroine's Journey: Woman's Guide to Wholeness*, 32. Murdock quotes Jill Barad, the executive vice-president of marketing for Mattel Toys who gave an interview for the Los Angeles Times. LA Times Magazine, "The Southern California Woman, On the Job, Making it, The Personal Stories of Six Women Who Have Found Success in Individual Ways: Jill Barad, Corporation Executive," *Los Angeles Times* 4 December 1988. http://articles.latimes.com/1988-12-04/magazine/tm-1687 _1_jill-barad. She eventually became CEO and chairperson.
14. Murdock, *The Heroine's Journey: Woman's Guide to Wholeness*, 32.
15. Murdock, *The Heroine's Journey: Woman's Guide to Wholeness*, 41.
16. Neumann, *Amor*, 8.
17. Brontë, *Jane Eyre*, 99.
18. Brontë, *Jane Eyre*, 108.
19. Brontë, *Jane Eyre*, 8–9.
20. Brontë, *Jane Eyre*, 13.
21. Brontë, *Jane Eyre*.
22. Murdock, *The Heroine's Journey: Woman's Guide to Wholeness*, 46.
23. Murdock, *The Heroine's Journey: Woman's Guide to Wholeness*, 47.
24. Murdock, *The Heroine's Journey: Woman's Guide to Wholeness*, 48.
25. Brontë, *Jane Eyre*, 111.
26. Brontë, *Jane Eyre*, 113.
27. Brontë, *Jane Eyre*, 114.
28. Brontë, *Jane Eyre*, 129.

29. C. G. Jung, *"The Structure and Dynamics of the Psyche,"* in *Collected Works,* ed. Herbert Read et al., *The Collected Works of C. G. Jung,* vol. 8 (2nd, Princeton: Princeton University Press, 1969), 345.

30. *Titanic.*

31. Ibid.

32. Murdock, *The Heroine's Journey: Woman's Guide to Wholeness,* 61; Campbell, *Hero,* 172–92.

33. Apuleius and Ruden, *The Golden Ass,* 106.

34. Brontë, *Jane Eyre,* 307.

35. Brontë, *Jane Eyre,* 314.

36. Brontë, *Jane Eyre,* 314.

37. Murdock, *The Heroine's Journey: Woman's Guide to Wholeness,* 71; Campbell, *Hero.*

38. Murdock, *The Heroine's Journey: Woman's Guide to Wholeness,* 71 & 74.

39. Murdock, *The Heroine's Journey: Woman's Guide to Wholeness,* 85.

40. Gisela Labouvie-Vief, *Psyche and Eros: Mind and Gender in the Life Course* (Cambridge, New York: Cambridge University Press, 1994), 162–63.

41. Cameron, *Screenplay,* 65.

42. Cameron, *Screenplay,* 74.

43. Cameron, *Screenplay.*

44. Murdock, *The Heroine's Journey: Woman's Guide to Wholeness,* 87–88.

45. Marie-Louise von Franz, *The Feminine in Fairy Tales,* Rev. ed. (Boston, New York: Shambhala, 1993), 106.

46. Samuel Noah Kramer, *The Sumerians: Their History, Culture, and Character* (Chicago: University of Chicago Press, 1963), 85.

47. Samuel Noah Kramer, *Sumerian Mythology: A Study of Spiritual and Literary Achievement in the Third Millennium B.C,* Rev. ed. (New York: Harper, 1961), 64. The decrees, known as *mes,* were given to her in fourteen sets and includes mandates relating to her authority as goddess, queen, priestess, her symbols of sovereignty, capacities as a priestess, accoutrements of royalty, dominion over sex and reproduction, various arts of good and evil, assorted crafts, powers of perception, advocacy, compassion, empathy, judgment, and decisivness. Diane Wolkstein and Samuel Noah Kramer, *Inanna, Queen of Heaven and Earth: Her Stories and Hymns from Sumer* (New York: Harper & Row, 1983), 16–18.

48. Murdock, *The Heroine's Journey: Woman's Guide to Wholeness,* 88.

49. Hamilton, *Mythology,* 45; Johnson, *She,* 50.

50. Apuleius, *Cupid & Psyche,* ed. E. J. Kenney (Cambridge, New York: Cambridge University Press, 1990), 74.

51. Brontë, *Jane Eyre,* 390.

52. Brontë, *Jane Eyre,* 391.

53. Brontë, *Jane Eyre.*

54. Brontë, *Jane Eyre,* 391.

55. Brontë, *Jane Eyre.*

56. Cameron, *Screenplay,* 105.

57. Franz, *The Feminine in Fairy Tales,* 99.

58. Kramer, *Sumerian Mythology: A Study of Spiritual and Literary Achievement in the Third Millennium B.C*, 92–93.

59. Wolkstein and Kramer, *Inanna, Queen of Heaven and Earth: Her Stories and Hymns from Sumer*.

60. Wolkstein and Kramer, *Inanna, Queen of Heaven and Earth: Her Stories and Hymns from Sumer*, 149.

61. Wolkstein and Kramer, *Inanna, Queen of Heaven and Earth: Her Stories and Hymns from Sumer*.

62. Wolkstein and Kramer, *Inanna, Queen of Heaven and Earth: Her Stories and Hymns from Sumer*, 160.

63. Lucius Apuleius, *Cupid & Psyche*, ed. E. J. Kenney (Cambridge & New York: Cambridge University Press, 1990), 91.

64. Apuleius and Ruden, *The Golden Ass*, 120.

65. Apuleius, *Cupid & Psyche*, 99.

66. Brontë, *Jane Eyre*, 394.

67. Brontë, *Jane Eyre*, 396.

68. Brontë, *Jane Eyre*, 402.

69. Cameron, *Screenplay*, 107.

70. Cameron, *Screenplay*, 108.

71. Cameron, *Screenplay*.

72. *Titanic*.

73. Cameron, *Screenplay*, 110.

74. Murdock, *The Heroine's Journey: Woman's Guide to Wholeness*, 110.

75. Murdock, *The Heroine's Journey: Woman's Guide to Wholeness*, 117.

76. Murdock, *The Heroine's Journey: Woman's Guide to Wholeness*, 120.

77. Murdock, *The Heroine's Journey: Woman's Guide to Wholeness*, 126.

78. Murdock, *The Heroine's Journey: Woman's Guide to Wholeness*, 127 and 28.

79. Apuleius, *Cupid & Psyche*.

80. Murdock, *The Heroine's Journey: Woman's Guide to Wholeness*, 128.

81. Franz, *Golden Ass*, 116.

82. Neumann, *Amor*, 96.

83. Apuleius, *Cupid & Psyche*, 101.

84. Neumann, *Amor*, 100; Franz, *Golden Ass*, 120; Johnson, *She*, 58.

85. Franz, *Golden Ass*, 118.

86. Franz, *Golden Ass*, 124; Neumann, *Amor*, 103.

87. Neumann, *Amor*, 103.

88. Brontë, *Jane Eyre*, 408.

89. Brontë, *Jane Eyre*, 411.

90. Cameron, *Screenplay*, 122.

91. Murdock, *The Heroine's Journey: Woman's Guide to Wholeness*, 139.

92. Brontë, *Jane Eyre*, 438.

93. Brontë, *Jane Eyre*, p. 413.

94. Brontë, *Jane Eyre*, 448.

95. Murdock, *The Heroine's Journey: Woman's Guide to Wholeness*, 156.

96. Murdock, *The Heroine's Journey: Woman's Guide to Wholeness*.

97. Murdock, *The Heroine's Journey: Woman's Guide to Wholeness*, 158.

98. Murdock, *The Heroine's Journey: Woman's Guide to Wholeness*, 160.

99. Wolkstein and Kramer, *Inanna, Queen of Heaven and Earth: Her Stories and Hymns from Sumer*, 165.

100. N.J. Girardot, "Initiation and Meaning in the Tale of Snow White and the Seven Dwarfs," *The Journal of American Folklore* 90, No. 357 (1977): 284.

101. Brontë, *Jane Eyre*, 500.

102. Brontë, *Jane Eyre*, 508.

103. Brontë, *Jane Eyre*, 512.

104. Brontë, *Jane Eyre*, 513.

105. Brontë, *Jane Eyre*, 514.

106. Brontë, *Jane Eyre*, 517.

107. Brontë, *Jane Eyre*, 530.

108. Brontë, *Jane Eyre*, 533.

109. "Mstislav Keldysh Family History," accessed September 6, 2017, <http://www.famhist.ru/famhist/schelkin/0006952a.htm>.

110. Isabelle Clark, "The Gamos of Hera," in *The Sacred and The Feminine in Ancient Greece*, ed. Sue Blundell and Margaret Williamson (London & New York: Routledge, 1998), 13.

111. Murdock, *The Heroine's Journey: Woman's Guide to Wholeness*, 160.

112. Martin Lowenthal, *Alchemy of the Soul: The Eros and Psyche Myth as a Guide to Transformation* (Berwick: Nicolas-Hays, 2004), 148–49.

113. Neumann, *Amor*, 52.

114. Neumann, *Amor*, 145.

115. C. G. Jung, "*Symbols of Transformation: An Analysis of the Prelude to a Case of Schizophrenia*," ed. Herbert Read et al., *The Collected Works of C. G. Jung*, vol. 5 (2nd, New York: Harper, 1962), 433.

116. Brontë, *Jane Eyre*, 552.

117. Brontë, *Jane Eyre*.

118. C. G. Jung, "*Psychology and Class of Religion: West and East*," ed. Herbert Read et al., *The Collected Works of C. G. Jung*, vol. 11 (Princeton: Princeton University Press, 1969), 72.

119. Cameron, *Screenplay*, 152.

120. Murdock, *The Heroine's Journey: Woman's Guide to Wholeness*, 161.

121. Neumann, *Amor*, 140.

122. Brontë, *Jane Eyre*, 553.

123. James Horner and Céline Dion, "My Heart Will Go On (Love Theme From Titanic)," in *Titanic Music from the Motion Picture* (New York: Sony Classical, 1997), sound recording.

124. Horner and Dion, "My Heart Will Go On (Love Theme From Titanic)."

Chapter 6

On the Transmodern Monomyth
A Critical Perspective

As an American with ethnic origins hailing from Latin America, I was born and educated in the global north on a heritage from the global south. I am particularly conscious of the critique of the hero's journey as a western force of cultural imperialism. Is my global north side attempting to conquer my global south side through hegemonic story? Once the vanguard of modernism, hegemony fell into disfavor with postmodernism as an emblem of the failure of universal truths. Thus, Joseph Campbell, *the* proponent of the universal story, became a dinosaur of a bygone era—or so he should have, by all accounts, except for George Lucas. Was George Lucas then as much of an imperialist as Darth Vader or did he represent a supernatural force in support of a rebel thought from alterity?

In *The History of Western Philosophy*, Bertrand Russell argues that the "modern epoch" began as early as Rene Descartes's egocentric declaration "I think, therefore I am," separating truth from external authority and ushering in a period of Enlightenment that favored rational over religious thought.[1] The certainty of science, aided by the Scientific Revolution, eroded the influence of belief in unproven dogma. Historical understanding was replaced by a scientific method based on doubtless axiomatic, universal principles that would enable any thinker to arrive at truth. As Descartes notes, "In our search for the direct road to truth, we should not occupy ourselves with any object about which we are unable to have a certitude equal to that of arithmetical and geometrical demonstrations."[2] While Immanuel Kant sought to explicate a universal morality, he defined Enlightenment "as the human being's emancipation from self-incurred immaturity" understanding that self-inflicted immaturity arises when a person lacks the "resolve and courage to make use of one's intellect without the direction of another."[3] Society shifted from a focus on public to personal welfare, a move away from the ancients towards moderns, from the village to the city, from the provincial to the cosmopolitan.

101

Kant wrote for the "Idea of a Universal History from a Cosmopolitan" on the theory of equality between all people, as rational beings.[4] Secularism arose as the foundation of the cosmopolitan ideal and the antidote to religious intolerance that afflicted the eighteenth-century West with strife in the name of God, as state separated from Church and democracy flourished. This led Alexis de Tocqueville to comment about democracy in America that "nothing struck me more forcibly than the general equality of condition among people" and then conclude that "the gradual development of the principle of equality is a providential fact. It has all the chief characteristics of such a fact: it is universal, it is durable, it constantly eludes all human interference, and all events as well as all men contribute to its progress."[5] As a consequence, according to historian and social critic Christopher Lasch, "The assumption of uniformity sometimes gave rise to sweeping reforms untempered by the slightest doubt about the ability of enlightened legislators to prescribe for all. Armed with a scientific understanding of the requirements of happiness, philanthropists like Jeremy Bentham did not hesitate to propose a comprehensive reconstruction of political institutions, in which all the errors allowed to accumulate during the unenlightened ages past—errors undeservedly dignified as ancestral wisdom—would be ruthlessly swept aside."[6]

Science and reason surpassed faith and tradition as the guiding principle of progress. Advancement in technology reinforced the conviction that application of the intellect improved human life, freeing it from historical baggage and oppressive, traditional institutions. The promise of modernity, as fueled by Enlightenment philosophy inspired progress in the West until the twentieth-century. However, certain events began to erode the belief in science and the inevitability of progress brought about by democratic institutions, chief among them relating to the loss of certainty in mathematics. According to Professor Morris Kline, who wrote extensively on the history and philosophy of mathematics, "By 1800, mathematics was in a highly paradoxical situation. Its successes in representing and predicting physical phenomena were beyond all expectation superlative. On the other hand, as many eighteenth-century men had already pointed out, the massive structure had no logical foundation, and there was no assurance that mathematics was correct."[7] In 1931, Kurt Gödel inadvertently upended the core of liberal thought by discovering a mathematical theorem that establishes the enduring uncertainty of mathematics.[8] "[T]he pride of man—is a grand illusion."[9]

That was not the only setback to modernism. Equality proved exclusive. Up until 1920, women were denied the equal right to vote. The constitutional promise of liberty and justice for all failed its Black citizens in the Jim Crow Era. In 1909, W. E. B. Du Bois established the National Association for the Advancement of Colored People (NAACP), which began a half century of litigation and lobbying campaigns against disenfranchisement, lynching, and racial segregation. World wars were fought in the name of democracy without the foregone, anticipated successes. Disenchantment bled into the culture. The pursuit of modernist ideals at the cost of excluding diversity became less and less tenable. As the authors of the *Dialectics of Enlightenment*, Mark Horkheimer and Theodor W. Adorno remarked, "On the way from mythology to logistics, thought has lost the element of self-reflection."[10]

Into this time, Joseph Campbell composes *The Hero with a Thousand Faces* in the mid-century as an indictment against modernity's isolating effect on a person; severing humanity from tradition was a mistake to be rectified with a return to mythology. In his conclusion, he argues, "All of which is far indeed from the contemporary view; for the democratic ideal of the self-determining individual, the invention of the power-driven machine, and the development of the scientific method of research, has so transformed human life that the long-inherited, timeless universe of symbols has collapsed."[11] He decries the use of reason that produces knowledge without real wisdom. Writing in reference to Friedrich Nietzsche's "murderous criticism" of current universities in which Nietzsche stated, "There is nothing from which this culture suffers more than from superabundance of pretentious corner-watchers and fragments of humanity; and the universities, against their will, are the real hothouses of this kind of stunting of the spiritual instincts." Campbell adds:

"[G]reat books" summarized and evaluated, stuffed into emptied heads as authorized information, to be signaled back, for grades; and then the sciences—at the outer reaches of thought!—all taught by sterilized authorities who, in those unrecapturable years of their own youth, when the ears, eyes, and heart of the spirit open to the marvel of oneself and the universe, were condemned to that same hard helotism of which Nietzsche writes. There is no time, no place, no permission—let alone encouragement—for experience. And to make things even worse, along now come those possessed sociopolitical maniacs with their campus rallies, picket-line slogans, journalistic ballyhoo, and summonses to action in the name of causes of which their callow flocks had scarcely heard six months before—and even those marginal hours that might have been left from study for inward growth are invaded, wrecked, and strewn with daily rubbish. It is hardly to be wondered if the young people of the world today look a bit like rubbish-strewn rooms themselves and in their Dionysiac "trips" and "happenings" promise to match the *agapes* of the early Christian Church.[12]

Campbell appeals to a future hero to rise and rescue society from modernity by heeding intuition and the cry for symbols. In that sense, however, postmodern cultural critics mistake Campbell's appeal as advocating for "rugged individualism," particularly scrutinizing Hollywood's essentialization of the hero as an American rugged individualist which in turn has been misappropriated by media imperialism.[13] Nonetheless, nearly thirty years later, George

Lucas would become Campbell's hero, having discovered a novel manner to incorporate ancient symbols into contemporary life without upending modern institutions or reverting to antiquated traditions.

In the interim, however, Campbell's call to action could not rise above the din of postmodern thinkers such as Jean-Francois Lyotard, Michel Foucault, Martin Heidegger, and Jacques Derrida, who cast doubt on universalisms and introduced an age of cynicism. Postmodernism rejects modernity and its totalizing, grand narratives, which had generally attempted to apply "objective" solutions to rationalized social problems, resulting in a plethora of ideologies such as liberalism, capitalism, anarchism, socialism, fascism, Stalinism, and others. Modernist ideals spoke only for a homogenous society using metanarratives to legitimize its power and turning a blind eye to its heterogeneity. After witnessing the numerous crimes against humanity that occurred during World War II and through colonization, society became skeptical of totalizing ideologies and the acts it might authorize, while scholars assailed objective concepts such as reason, human nature, social progress, truth, and reality. Postmodern thinkers argued that structures of power did not represent egalitarian principles or service for a greater good. Rather, structures of power marginalized and disadvantaged the powerless with the sole purpose of consolidating and preserving its own authority.

Foucault, for example, argued that knowledge wasn't created in an objective vacuum of scientific thought. It exists in association with a structure of power that upholds it. "There is no power relation without the correlative constitution of a field of knowledge, nor any knowledge that does not presuppose and constitute at the same time power relations."[14] As a result, knowledge is deemed historically contingent, not universal. Language itself was suspect and open to varied, conflicting interpretations. Derrida deconstructed language to expose underlying biases of race, gender, religion, and class. A binary in language (for example, mankind refers to all of humanity, while womankind is a subset, infusing "man" with a norm and "woman" with deviation) could lead to biases in the knowledge produced about that topic. In essence, if language is imperfect, what sort of perfect conclusions could it have ever produced? In the absence of truths, then, any claims to knowledge are necessarily relative to the perspective of the claimant and their context and positionality. The postmodern perspective has been incorporated into the fields of journalism, law, and education resulting in advocacy journalism, political correctness, critical race theory, race and gender politics, and multiculturalism.

Patriarchy in particular has been critiqued as a structure of power that subjugated and exploited women. As Gerda Lerner, author of *The Creation of Patriarchy*, maintains, "Patriarchy in its wider definition means the manifestation and institutionalization of male dominance over women and children in the family and the extension of male dominance over women in society in general."[15] Centuries of Western patriarchy dating back to Aristotle who viewed women as biologically inferior intertextually undergirds twentieth-century psychology and Freud's theory of castration anxiety.[16] Men represent what women lack. Not surprisingly, such an imbalanced view may have triggered second-wave feminism after Simone de Beauvoir wrote *The Second Sex*, which articulated a long, overdue feminist account of the treatment of women in history, criticizing the definition of humanity as male.[17] "[M]an defines woman not in herself but as relative to him; she is not regarded as an autonomous being."[18] Beauvoir further explains that "One is not born, but rather becomes, a woman."[19] In contradistinction, Campbell reveals the limits of his authority when he claims that a girl "becomes a woman whether she intends it or not but the little boy has to intend to be a man."[20] When he says this in an interview with Bill Moyers in 1988 in *The Power of Myth*, he strikes a discordant note with feminists and essentializes the monomyth as a male journey.[21] "The boy first has to disengage himself from his mother, get his energy into himself, and then start forth," where as a girl does not.[22]

In postmodern feminism, Judith Butler critically reverts to Simone de Beauvoir to incorporate sex into a postmodern discourse on gender.[23] "[I]t appears that the female body is the arbitrary locus of the gender 'woman,' and there is no reason to preclude the possibility of that body becoming the locus of other constructions of gender."[24] In the same vein that there are no truths, there can be no truths about sex or gender. Sex and gender are social constructs. "If the immutable character of sex is contested, perhaps this construct called 'sex' is as culturally constructed as gender; indeed, perhaps it was always already gender, with the consequence that the distinction between sex and gender turns out to be no distinction at all."[25] As such, gender (and sex) is purely performative.[26]Adopting a certain amount of "feminist skepticism toward postmodernism," Seyla Benhabib argues that Butler's dilution of gender undermines "women's sense of selfhood, agency and autonomy" and that the gendered-self must exist because fundamentally performance does not exist without a subject.[27] Divesting the meaning of woman of its relevance to women is a kind of violence of its own.

Postmodernism has been further critiqued as a "Eurocentric critique of Eurocentrism" by the theorists from the periphery who don't share a history with the Enlightenment.[28] British-Pakistani postmodernism critic, Ziauddin Sardar, asserts further that:

[P]ostmodernism, from the perspective of the Other, the non-western cultures, is simply a new wave of domination riding on the crest of colonialism and modernity [. . .]. Postmodern relativism embraces the Other, making alterity far more than just the representation of all non-western cultures and societies. Alterity is the condition of difference in any binary pair of differences; there is even alterity within the self. [But] instead of finally doing justice to the marginalized and demeaned, it vaunts the category to prove how unimportant, and ultimately meaningless, is any real identity it could contain. We are all Others now, can appropriate the Other, consume artefacts of the Other, so what does it matter if Others want something different in their future [. . .].[29]

If everything, including "Others," is relative, then as the songwriter Freddie Mercury quite memorably celebrated, "nothing really matters" except, however, for what the market implicitly dictates to matter.[30] For instance, despite the aforementioned lyrics, "Bohemian Rhapsody" clearly mattered to a lot of people becoming the top British single of all time, the most streamed song from the twentieth century, and the oldest music video to reach a billion views on YouTube.[31] By the same logic, no story matters, but in fact the movies put out by Hollywood, as evidenced by the box office numbers, matter. Relativism is belied by the fact that some narratives, whether sung, heard, watched, played, or read, still matter more than others. The "Bohemian Rhapsody" is ultimately a Dionysian song.

In rejecting the Cartesian dualistic framework arising from the mind/body dichotomy, postmodernism, characterized by skepticism, relativism, and a focus on the power of language to create reality, emerged as a critique of these foundational assumptions. Despite objections to binary thinking, postmodernism takes shape as an opposing force to modernism, creating a new binary. While questioning the authority of dominant narratives in the interest of inclusion, postmodernism argues from a center/margin binary. While deconstructionism destabilizes binaries to unearth artificial or constructed origins, it exists in the context of binaries. Does text hold any fixed, intrinsic meaning as originally supposed, or does the reader create meaning through the act of reading—another binarism between the text and reader?

Postmodernism reminds us of the problem of the absolutist ends of dualistic thought, which has enabled structures of power to oppress.[32] Therefore, all binaries are viewed with suspicion, fundamentally flawed. However, this is also a form of absolutism. Not all dichotomies are absolute, and it's important to examine the ways in which what was previously considered as polarizing opposites could be seen as more complementary pairs of a whole unit. Postmodernism essentializes dualism as a mere function of extremes, negating the complexities and fluidity found in a dynamic coupling. Such an approach contributes to the muting of a heroine's journey under an assumption that it refers to a social, and by implication irrelevant, construct, allowing us to adopt a certain deafness to the journey of "Others."

Opining upon the inevitable trajectory of postmodern thought, Freidrich Nietzsche had predicted that, reasoned to its rational ends, postmodernism would veer towards nihilism, relativism, and anarchism. "Nihilism represents the ultimate logical conclusion of our great values and ideals."[33] In his posthumously published final book, *The Will to Power*, he stresses that "For some time now, our whole European culture has been moving as toward a catastrophe, with a tortured tension that is growing from decade to decade: restlessly, violently, headlong, like a river that wants to reach the end, that no longer reflects, that is afraid to reflect."[34] He concludes this four book series by referring back to the Apollonian and Dionysian writings from his first book, *The Birth of Tragedy*, wherein he argued for humanity's cure in tragedy via a return to a Primordial Unity as represented by the two antithetical Greek gods of Apollo and Dionysus.[35] For Nietzsche, the Enlightenment adopted an Apollonian approach to life by focusing on "Principle Individuation" to the exclusion of a Dionysian approach, which sought a "drunken" immersion with the whole.[36] He criticizes Socrates for having started the obsession with instrumental rationality that ultimately leads to involution. In prescient anticipation of Kurt Gödel's Incompleteness Theorem, Nietzsche decried the limits of science:

> But now science, spurred on by its powerful illusion, hastens irresistibly to its limits, on which its optimism, hidden in the essence of logic, is wrecked. For the periphery of the circle of science has an infinite number of points, and while there is still no telling how this circle can ever be completely measured, yet the noble and gifted man, even before the middle of his career, inevitably comes into contact with those extreme points of the periphery where he stares at the inexplicable. When he here sees to his dismay how logic coils round itself at these limits and finally bites its own tail—then the new form of perception discloses itself, namely *tragic perception*, which, in order even to be endured, requires art as a safeguard and remedy.[37]

Nietzsche calls for "tragic perception" in the same vein that Joseph Campbell calls for a "tragic catharsis"—both relying upon Dionysian rituals as might be exposed through "tragic art."[38] Thus for Nietzsche, Apollo represents the supreme development of the ego as "the god of individuation" while "by the mystical cheer of Dionysus the spell of individuation is broken, and the way lies open to the Mothers of Being, to the innermost heart of things."[39] I would only add that the spell of individuation for the first half of life is thereby broken. Writing at the end of his life, Nietzsche reminds us that the term "Apollinian [sic]" refers to "the urge to perfect self-sufficiency, to the typical 'individual,' to all that simplifies, distinguishes, makes strong, clear, unambiguous, typical: freedom under the law."[40] The "Dionysian" refers to "an urge to unity, a reaching out beyond personality, the everyday, society, reality, across the abyss of transitoriness: a passionate-painful overflowing into darker, fuller, more floating states."[41] The Dionysian is "the eternal will to procreation, to fruitfulness, to recurrence; the feeling of the necessary unity of creation and destruction."[42] Apollo is the hero, Dionysus the heroine of a lived life (notwithstanding the fact that he's gendered male in mythology). By incorporating Dionysus into the Apollonian modernist life, one might understand:

> [T]he final mysteries of the "destiny of the soul" [. . .] to rediscover the South in one and to spread out above one a bright, glittering, mysterious southern sky; to re-conquer southern health and hidden powerfulness of soul; step by step to become more comprehensive, more supranational, more European, more Near Eastern, finally more Greek—for the Greek was the first great union and synthesis of everything Near Eastern, and on that account the inception of the European soul, the discovery of our "new world."[43]

Campbell believed in the truth of mythologies to reach and teach the soul how to thrive in a profane world and agreed with Nietzsche on the necessity of tragedy to create a catharsis, which he believed to be the function of Dionysus.[44] In this vein, Campbell couldn't be considered a postmodernist. As Joseph Felser notes, "Campbell could never have accepted the postmodern view that there are virtually no genuinely objective, culturally transcendent, linguistically or conceptually independent constraints on the (in principle) endless process of redescribing ourselves and our world for the simple reason that he believed that human beings possess an essential spiritual nature whose imperative cannot be denied, except at great cost and peril to individual and collective alike."[45]

Psychoanalyst and philosopher Julia Kristeva paves a way for a path beyond postmodernism.[46] She coined the term "intertextuality" to suggest that a text never stands alone but acts and reacts in dialogue with other texts as part of a larger cultural, historical, and linguistic context that carries echoes of other writings within it.[47] For Kristeva, a text draws on the semiotic and the symbolic to create and recreate cultural and linguistic traditions embedded within it, where the semiotic applies to the pre-Oedipal, rhythmic, and nonverbal elements of communication while the symbolic references the socially accepted, linear structure of language. The emphasis here is not to discard any rational framework to language but to incorporate its nonvocal, unstructured parts as an integral, coequal, and complementary factor. Kristeva also discusses the "other" in the context of the "self," where the self is familiar while the other is the projected "feeling of uncanny strangeness," a repression of what's recognizable by the mind but alienated.[48] Echoing Enrique Dussel's transmodernism, she claims:

My discontent in living with the other—my strangeness, his strangeness—rests on the perturbed logic that governs this strange bundle of drive and language, of nature and symbol, constituted by the unconscious, always already shaped by the other. It is through unraveling transference—the major dynamics of otherness, of love/hatred for the other, of the foreign component of our psyche—that, on the basis of the other, I become reconciled with my own otherness-foreignness, that I play on it and live by it. Psychoanalysis is then experienced as a journey into the strangeness of the other and of oneself, toward an ethics of respect for the irreconcilable. How could one tolerate a foreigner if one did not know one was a stranger to oneself?[49]

In Nietzschean terms, moving past postmodernism requires a return to Dionysus, an embrace of tragedy, a catharsis, heteronomous emersion, or a release of conscious will—in Jungian terms, a reunion with the unconscious. For Emmanuel Levinas, this is a turn to the inclusion of the Other. Levinas argues that, philosophically, truth can be pursued along two separate routes, autonomy and heteronomy, a dichotomy of *same* versus *other*, but, historically, truth has been presumptively pursued for autonomous (Apollonian) egoistic ends. The latter is problematic for Levinas because:

This consciousness is not concerned with situating itself relative to an exteriority, does not grasp itself as part of a whole (for it precedes all grasping); it is a consciousness without consciousness to which the term the unconscious (which covers over no fewer contradictions) or instinct corresponds. The inwardness which, for a thinking being, is opposed to exteriority, occurs in a living being as an absence of exteriority. There is nothing mysterious in the identity of a living being throughout its history: it is essentially the same, the same determining every other, without the other ever determining it.[50]

From a monomythic perspective, this is the exercise of the hero's journey to the exclusion of the heroine's journey, on a patriarchal, Apollonian presumption of sameness for all. Same denotes the self (not in a Jungian sense, but a Levinasian sense of self) and all attempts to reduce what is familiar to the same, while the other refers to all that is beyond the self, incomprehensible, alterior. The other is exterior and infinitely beyond the totality of being. In the name of autonomy, the threat presented by the other is neutralized by domination, colonization, conquest, and possession, reducing all experiences to a "universal synthesis" of the same.[51]

Marginalized peoples, exteriorized by the totalizing system of Western hegemony based on race, religion, sex, ethnicity, nationalism, and other divisions, have been stepping forward for recognition and justice not as part of a civilizing rehabilitation to become part of the same (postmodernism) but to be emancipated from totalization (transmodernism). For Levinas, justice in

such circumstances occurs in the face-to-face encounter between the same
and the other as part of their mutual ethical responsibility for humanity. In a
true meeting between them an epiphany occurs. "This gaze that supplicates
and demands, that can supplicate only because it demands, deprived of
everything because entitled to everything, and which one recognizes in giving (as one 'puts the things in question in giving')--this gaze is precisely the
epiphany of the face as a face."[52] Before the voice of reason can be heard in
the face-to-face moment between self and other, between north and south, a
voice is heard, the semiotic precedes the symbolic. Transmodern philosopher
Enrique Dussel develops this further:

> I called this "ethical-preoriginary reason." "Ethical-preoriginary reason" is the
> first rational moment, prior to any other use of reason, by virtue of which we
> have the experience (empirical and material, which makes it the same as the
> "practical-material reason") of responsibility-for-the-Other. This experience
> occurs prior to any decision, commitment, linguistic expression or communica-
> tion about the Other. "Ethical-preoriginary reason" allows us to be stirred by an
> "obsession" or "responsibility for the Other." This responsibility is a priori. It is
> always presupposed by any propositional or argumentative linguistic expression
> in every communication, in every consensus or agreement, in every praxis.[53]

Influenced by Levinas, Dussel argues for transmodernism in order to move
past exclusionary discourse. "From this omitted potentiality and altering
'exteriority' emerges a project of 'trans'-modernity, a 'beyond' that transcends Western modernity (since the West has never adopted it but, rather,
has scorned it and valued it as 'nothing') and that will have a creative function of great significance in the twenty-first century."[54] In reference to the
postcolonial challenge towards modernity's impact upon colonized societies, "I call the reality of that fertile multicultural moment 'trans'-modernity
(since 'post'-modernity is just the latest moment of Western modernity)."[55]
Transmodern theory arises as a disruption of postmodernism, an intervention
from the global south for inclusion from the margins through a "plurality of
horizons that transcend modernity" in order "to open a dialogue of mutual
respect of differences."[56] According to Dussel, "*Trans-modernity* is a task
that is, in my case, expressed philosophically, whose point of departure is
that which has been *discarded, devalued*, and judged *useless* among global
cultures, including colonized or peripheral philosophies."[57] One point of
departure references the philosophical Cartesian egocentric male Western
view of *ego cogito*. Global south thinkers take issue with the presumption of
the supremacy of the ego above all else, including God. Ramon Grosfoguel
contends that this reflects a separation of the mind and body, the ego-politics

knowledge of the global north versus a body-politics knowledge of the global south.[58]

From a post-Jungian perspective, to the extent that the Ego (as in consciousness) is developed without regard to the Self (as in the unconscious), it inherently overinflates. When the Ego, as driven by the masculine principle, however, allows the polarity of the Self, as driven by the feminine principle, to act upon it in an "analectical moment,"[59] a symbiotic balance can be achieved psychically, and, as Campbell would argue, sociologically and cosmologically. Under transmodern theory, the egolatric Western approach needs to incorporate knowledge of the exteriority of the Other, which in this case is the unconscious. By this definition, the monomyth, when retooled to reflect a coming of age (ego separation in the hero's journey) and a coming of middle age (ego re-integration in the heroine's journey), representing a global north and global south face-to-face discourse, exemplifies a transmodern theory in a pluriverse of interconnected and intertextual diverse heroisms. The hero's journey has been a universalizing, totalizing, patriarchal, Apollonian story of conquer in the name of autonomy. The heroine's journey, which can also be found indigenously in the global north and south, is a pluriversal, alterior, matriarchal, Dionysian story of surrender in the name of heteronomy. Mythopoesis provides that middle ground between subjective and objective reality as the depersonalized lived experience. It speaks *a* truth but it doesn't speak *all* truth. It doesn't universalize the lived experience. It only universalizes *a* lived experience in *a* moment of time. In that way, perhaps we can bridge the gap between subject and object, the egocentric autonomous and the sociocentric organic, the global north and the global south—a mythopoeic moment in a lived experience. The joining of the Apollonian and Dionysian, the hero and the heroine, as in the rebooted monomyth results in a Jungian syzygy or Dusselian epiphany in a Levinasian face-to-face encounter of an analectical moment.

NOTES

1. Bertrand Russell, *History of Western Philosophy and Its Connection with Political and Social Circumstances from the Earliest Times to the Present Day* (London: G. Allen and Unwin ltd, 1946), 513.

2. R. Descartes and N.K. Smith, *Descartes Philosophical Writings* (New York: Modern Library, 1958), 29. A statement that laters proves to be false by the mathematical proofs of Kurt Gödel.

3. Immanuel Kant et al., *Toward Perpetual Peace and Other Writings on Politics, Peace, and History* (New Haven: Yale University Press, 2006), 18.

4. Kant et al., *Toward Perpetual Peace and Other Writings on Politics, Peace, and History*, 28.

5. Alexis De Tocqueville, *Democracy in America*, trans. Henry Reeve, ed. Francis Bowen (London: Wordsworth, 1998), 7–8.

6. Christopher Lasch, *The True and Only Heaven: Progress and Its Critics* (New York: W.W. Norton & Company, 1991), 127.

7. Morris Kline, *Mathematics: The Loss of Certainty* (New York: Oxford University Press, 1980), 153.

8. See Ernest Nagel and James Roy Newman, *Gödel's Proof* (New York: New York University Press, 1958).

9. Kline, *Mathematics: The Loss of Certainty*, 6.

10. Max Horkheimer and Theodor W. Adorno, *Dialectic of Enlightenment*, trans. Edmund Jephcott (Stanford: Stanford University Press, 2002), 37.

11. Campbell, *The Hero with a Thousand Faces*, 333. All quotes from Joseph Campbell's *The Hero with a Thousand Faces* Copyright © Joseph Campbell Foundation (jcf.org) 2008. Used with permission.

12. Joseph Campbell, *The Masks of God: Creative Mythology*, 4 vols. (New York: Arkana, 1991), 374.

13. Sarah E. Bond and Joel Christensen, "The Man Behind the Myth: Should We Question the Hero's Journey," *LA Review of Books* (https://lareviewofbooks.org/article/the-man-behind-the-myth-should-we-question-the-heros-journey/), August 12, 2021. See also, Lawrence M. Eppard et al., *Rugged Individualism and the Misunderstanding of American Inequality* (Bethlehem: Lehigh University Press, 2020). The authors argue that the American cultural sentiment espousing President Herbert Hoover's conception of "rugged individualism" has disparately impacted the poor. See also, Edward W. Said, *Culture and Imperialism* (New York: Vintage Books, 1994). By essentializing Campbell's hero, Hollywood perpetuates the disempowering myth of individualism globally.

14. Michel Foucault, *Discipline and Punish: The Birth of the Prison*, trans. Alan Sheridan, 2nd ed. (New York: Vintage Books, 1995), 27.

15. Gerda Lerner, *The Creation of Patriarchy* (New York: Oxford University Press, 1986), 239.

16. Lerner, *The Creation of Patriarchy*, 19 and 206–07.

17. Beauvoir, *The Second Sex*, xliv.

18. Beauvoir, *The Second Sex*, xliv.

19. Beauvoir, *The Second Sex*, 281.

20. Joseph Campbell and Bill D. Moyers, *The Power of Myth* (New York: Doubleday, 1988), 168.

21. Campbell and Moyers, *The Power of Myth*, 168.

22. Campbell and Moyers, *The Power of Myth*, 168.

23. Judith Butler, "Sex and Gender in Simone de Beauvoir's 'Second Sex,'" *Yale French Studies* 72 (1987).

24. Butler, "Sex and Gender in Simone de Beauvoir's 'Second Sex,'" 35.

25. Butler, *Gender Trouble: Feminism and the Subversion of Identity*, 21.

26. Butler, *Gender Trouble: Feminism and the Subversion of Identity*, 25.

27. Seyla Benhabib, *Situating the Self: Gender, Community, and Postmodernism in Contemporary Ethics* (New York: Routledge, 1992), 213–16.

28. Walter D. Mignolo, "The Geopolitics of Knowledge and the Colonial Difference," *The South Atlantic Quarterly* 101, no. 1 (2002): 57, https://doi.org/10.1215/00382876-101-1-57. Mignolo notes that Enrique Dussel's response to the question of "What else can there be, beyond a Eurocentric critique of modernity and Eurocentrism?" is transmodern theory.

29. Ziauddin Sardar, *Postmodernism and the Other: The New Imperialism of Western Culture* (London, Sterling: Pluto Press, 1998), 13.

30. Queen, "Bohemian Rhapsody," *A Night at the Opera* (EMI, 1975).

31. Simon Thompson, "Queen's 'Bohemian Rhapsody' is Officially the World's Most-Streamed Song," *Forbes*, December 10, 2018, https://www.forbes.com/sites/simonthompson/2018/12/10/queens-bohemian-rhapsody-is-officially-the-worlds-most-streamed-song/?sh=6b14c1bcc1f0; Ben Beaumont-Thomas, "Queen's Bohemian Rhapsody Becomes Most Streamed Song from the 20th Century," *The Guardian*, December 11, 2018, https://www.theguardian.com/music/2018/dec/11/queen-bohemian-rhapsody-most-streamed-song-20th-century; "Queen's 'Bohemian Rhapsody' Becomes Oldest Music Video to Get a Billion YouTube Views," *Variety*, https://variety.com/2019/music/news/queen-bohemian-rhapsody-video-youtube-billion-record-1203275069/.

32. For instance, in the moral question of good versus evil, certain actions are seen as absolutely good while others are absolutely evil. In principle then, the absolute good is entitled to trump absolute evil or just evil. See Max Horkheimer and Theodor W. Adorno, *Dialectic of Enlightenment* (New York: Herder and Herder, 1972). Their central argument is that the the period in Western history where reason and individual liberty were championed (the absolute good), paradoxically led to new forms of oppression and domination. The Enlightenment's emphasis on rationality, while initially a progressive power against superstition and tradition (the presumptive evil), ultimately resulted in the dehumanization and alienation of individuals in marginalized groups.

33. Friedrich Wilhelm Nietzsche, *The Will to Power*, trans. R. J. Wilhelm Kaufmann and Walter Arnold Hollingdale (New York: Vintage Books, 1968), 3.

34. Nietzsche, *The Will to Power*, 3.

35. Friedrich Wilhelm Nietzsche, *The Birth of Tragedy; or Hellenism and Pessimism*, 3rd ed. (London: George Allen and Unwin Ltd, 1923), 27.

36. Nietzsche, *The Birth of Tragedy; or Hellenism and Pessimism*, 27–31.

37. Nietzsche, *The Birth of Tragedy; or Hellenism and Pessimism*, 119.

38. Campbell, *Hero*, 26.

39. Nietzsche, *The Birth of Tragedy; or Hellenism and Pessimism*, 80 and 121.

40. Nietzsche, *The Will to Power*, 539.

41. Nietzsche, *The Will to Power*, 539.

42. Nietzsche, *The Will to Power*, 539.

43. Nietzsche, *The Will to Power*, 541–42.

44. Campbell, *Hero*, 26.

45. Joseph M. Felser, "Was Joseph Campbell a Postmodernist," *Journal of the American Academy of Religion* 64, no. 2 (1996): 413–14.

46. Another perspective to explore in the course towards transmodernism would be the phenomenological philosophy of Maurice Merleau-Ponty (who sought to bridge the divide between phenomenolgy and existentialism), along with post-colonial works by Franz Fanon, Alia Al-Saji, and Linda Martin Alcoff that explore bodily otherness. Merleau-Ponty rejects Cartesian binarism of the mind and body, where the mind aspires to pure heights of truth beyond the reach of the profane body, and argues for the integral inclusion of the body as a source of knowledge. For Merleau-Ponty, knowledge derives from perception which is not simply a passive recipient of sensory information but an active, interpretative process grounded in the situated, embodied knowledge of lived experiences. See Maurice Merleau-Ponty, *Phenomenology of Perception* (London, New York: Routledge, 1962). The "intertextuality" of perception in the dynamic intercourse of the mind, body, and environment is what I call *intermentational* or *intermentationality*.

47. Julia Kristeva and Kelly Oliver, *The Portable Kristeva* (New York: Columbia University Press, 1997), 9 and 48.

48. Julia Kristeva, *Strangers to Ourselves* (New York: Columbia University Press, 1991), 184.

49. Kristeva, *Strangers to Ourselves*, 181–82.

50. Emmanuel Lévinas, *Collected Philosophical Papers*, trans. Alphonso Lingis, Phaenomenologica, (Dordrecht: Martinus Nijhoff Publishers, 1987), 26.

51. Emmanuel Lévinas, *Ethics and Infinity*, trans. Richard A. Cohen (Pittsburgh: Duquesne University Press, 1985), 75.

52. Emmanuel Lévinas, *Totality and Infinity: An Essay on Exteriority* (Pittsburgh: Duquesne University Press, 1969), 75.

53. Enrique D. Dussel, *Ethics of Liberation in the Age of Globalization and Exclusion*, trans. Alejandro A. Vallega (Durham: Duke University Press, 2013), 300.

54. Enrique Dussel, "World-System and 'Trans'-Modernity," *Nepantla* 3, no. 2 (2002): 221. There have been other scholars who have opined and defined this new moment of transmodernity. For a general discussion of those theorists, see Jessica Aliaga Lavrijsen and José María Yebra-Pertusa, eds., *Transmodern Perspectives on Contemporary Literatures in English* (New York: Routledge, 2019), 1–10.

55. Dussel, "World-System and 'Trans'-Modernity," 221.

56. Frederick B. Mills, *Enrique Dussel's Ethics of Liberation: An Introduction* (Cham: Palgrave Macmillan, 2018), 206.

57. Enrique Dussel, "A New Age in the History of Philosophy: The World Dialogue Between Philosophical Traditions," *Philosophy & Social Criticism* 35, no. 5 (2009): 514, https://doi.org/10.1177/0191453709103424.

58. Ramón Grosfoguel, "World-Systems Analysis in the Context of Transmodernity, Border Thinking, and Global Coloniality," *Review—Fernand Braudel Center for the Study of Economies, Historical Systems, and Civilizations* 29, no. 2 (2006): 168.

59. Enrique D. Dussel, *Philosophy of Liberation* (Maryknoll: Orbis Books, 1985), 158.

Chapter 7

On the Monomyth Rebooted

An Epilogue

In the Marvels' movie, *Avengers: Endgame*, the Avengers collectively and categorically defeat Thanos and those who were "snapped" return to life five years behind the times. But rather than simply taking Thanos's presence in the story literally, can it be viewed metaphorically—a battle between the life drive and the death drive, between Eros and Thanatos? Eros signifies the ego's journey of developing one's identity which occurs in the hero's journey. Thanatos indicates an end of things (making way for new beginnings) and an unwillingness to submit to Thanatos reveals a reluctance to put the ego to death for any reason, even if it means growth, insight, or deeper meaning. Ego above all, regardless of the consequences. This is perhaps what William Doty alluded to earlier when he asks, "How can it be that so much of our mass entertainment [. . .] is fixated at a teenage level of development?"[1] The monomythic fatigue experienced by the middle-aging *Star Wars'* generations (and the post *Star Wars* generations) is fueled in part by Christopher Vogler's sanitized divesture of some of its disagreeable portions to reduce the monomyth to a hero's journey but also, and perhaps mainly, because of a cultural defiance of the will to adult—a rage against middle age, a battle royale to conquer Thanatos. The ego trip will not end. The finale to the Avengers trilogy embeds the question in its title *Endgame*—a game of ends but for whom? It's revealing that the war between them is called the Infinity War—a totalizing war against knowledge of the sublime?

For Thanos to lose, the Avengers preserve the right of the ego to rule supreme, even if some returned behind the times—their development even further stunted. That's still better than actually facing the end, notwithstanding that it would allow for a new journey, for the ego to find its *self*. Even though the Avengers are victorious, culture suffers the greater loss to continue on ad infinitum in a bildungsroman hero's journey rather than embrace the age of the heroine in a künstlerroman. Ultimately, as noted by Jolande Jocabi,

"In the individuation process, as understood by Jung, the primary concern is the individual experience of 'death and rebirth' through struggle and suffering, through a conscious, lifelong, unremitting endeavor to broaden the scope of one's consciousness and so attain a greater inner freedom."[2] For Thanos to die and everyone to live, only one Avenger makes the ultimate sacrifice. There's a face-to-face moment in which Iron Man recognizes that to defeat death was to embrace it. In their final showdown, Thanos says, "I am inevitable," encapsulating his totalizing, authoritarian nature. Stark responds with, "And I am Iron Man,"[3] culminating his journey from a war profiteering, self-centered, "genius, billionaire, playboy, philanthropist," into a selfless superhero.[4] He slays his ego and gains an eternal union with the unconscious, saving the universe in the process, and perhaps signaling a future hope for a transmodern heroic rebirth in Tony Stark's young daughter.

Taken together, the hero and heroine's quests represent the experience of a mind's journey away from any socially constructed, polar, masculine and feminine extremes, sliding on a spectrum to various degrees of elected expression until it finds a balanced, androgyne center, which takes place by heroic exertion and surrender, not by passivity. In telling a story, the monomyth propounds activated human potential for internal peace. At a minimum, this narrative is constructed with twenty-four signposts on a continuum to affect an experience of wholeness by returning to a nascent, pre-conscious state with conscious awareness.

Storytellers have long, consciously or subconsciously, mythopoeically mined mythology to enrich their narrative with an eternal, possibly even sacred, consequence. Joseph Campbell took this further and recognized a mythic structure as a vehicle for hidden meaning from the unknown that enables a journeyer from anywhere to transcend beyond the immediate and knowable. But Campbell's description of the monomyth was academically flawed in areas. He asserted a theoretical mythological framework but moved at times inconsistently between Freud and Jung for justification, eventually settling on Jung but without fully accounting for Jungian psychology's application to his theory. He claimed his model could be found in many myths across different cultures but didn't map a single one against his seventeen stages. Rather, he steps back and allows the reader to pick and choose the milestones at random, promising that his monomyth endured regardless of his proof.

A closer inspection of analytical psychology especially with the benefit of postJungian theories reveals that the individuation process may in fact be viewed in heroic terms. In as much as individuation occurs in the two phases of life, coming of age and coming of middle age, then it calls upon two, separate, psychologically satisfying heroic journeys. The rebooted monomyth allows for the inclusion of both hero and heroine journeys as experienced on a spectrum from the socially constructed attributes of male to that of the female, swinging a symbolic pendulum of quests between the psychic masculine and feminine principles until the mind and heart has been centered, the Ego at one with the Self.

In the twenty-firstst century, the hero's journey, as abridged from the monomyth, has typified the colonizing masculine story of the global north, while the global south remains undiscovered and replete with heroine journeys. To move past postmodernism, as Nietzsche foresaw, we must "rediscover the South."[5] We might, for example, reconsider "Bohemian Rhapsody" from a global south, heroine's journey perspective. Freddie Mercury was originally Tanzanian of Parsi-Indian descent. Even in Muslim Zanzibar, he was a member of a minority of Zoroastrians. After gaining citizenship in the UK, he remained in the margins as a homosexual man. Bohemian Rhapsody in some respects is a gay anthem from alterity, chanting for a face-to-face recognition of LGBTQ humanity. The song begins with a Separation from the Maternal in describing the experience of being born: "Is this the real life? Is this just fantasy? Caught in a landslide" exiting the womb.[6] In Identification with the Paternal, Mercury says, "I'm just a poor boy" intertextually reminding us of another earlier famous song by Simon & Garfunkel, "The Boxer," about a poor boy whose story is seldom told.[7] "I need no sympathy" is Identification with the Paternal by rejecting what's feminine.[8] He embarks on the Road of Trials, which are "a little high, a little low."[9] He faces indecision as he allows himself to be lead without direction, "easy come, easy go."[10] He achieves an illusory Boon of success in killing "a man," in reference to his old self. But that success is temporary when he realizes that he'd just thrown away a good life, "life had just begun, but now I've gone and thrown it all away."[11] Thus, he Betrayed himself and his mother who begins to cry.

His Descent begins when his "time comes," sending "shivers down my spine."[12] He says, "goodbye everybody I've got go."[13] Then his Descent Dwelling begins when he has to "face the truth," knowing that he's dying, wishing he'd never been born, like Inanna whose lifeless body hung before the judges in the underworld, where he's become a "silhouette" of a man.[14] He takes on the costume of the court jester to dance the fandango as expressions of the Yearning to Reconnect with the feminine body through exercise and creative expression. He calls on Galileo, a man from Galilee, which can imply Jesus, repeating his name like a mantra. Thus, Mercury seeks metaphysical inspiration as he accounts for a betrayal from his boyhood. "Spare him his life from this monstrosity."[15] He heals the Mother-Child divide when he begs his mother to let him go. He finds a Man with a Heart in Beelzebub, here taken as a philistine god, whose saving him a devil, which he seems content with. There's Union in that he finds love ("so you think you can love me"), but then just as quickly he's dying.[16] In the end, "nothing really matters," reminding us of the final step of Bliss and Campbell's Freedom to Live, when, as Campbell contends, "there's a realization of the true relationship of the passing phenomena of time to the imperishable life that lives and dies in all."[17]

Another example of the heroine's journey in a global south story can be found in *Purple Hibiscus* by Chimamanda Ngozi Adichie, which follows the story of fifteen-year-old Kambili Achike from a wealthy family beset with domestic violence, in the Enugu State of a postcolonial Nigeria afflicted with economic straits and political instability.[18] From the outset, Kambili's mother suffers a miscarriage after a round of physical abuse from her father. Kambili's attempt to comfort her mother is rebuffed, and she suffers a Separation from the Mother at her inability to grieve with her mother who would rather grieve with the precious figurines that she doted on. Left to grieve alone, Kambili could only stare at her textbook instead of do homework. "The black type blurred, the letters swimming into one another, and then changed to a bright red, the red of fresh blood. The blood was watery, flowing from Mama, flowing from my eyes."[19] Kambili attends an elite, expensive school and wants to be number one, Overidentifying with her Father's ambition for his children. "I wanted to make Papa proud, to do as well as he had done. I needed him to touch the back of my neck and tell me that I was fulfilling God's purpose. I needed him to hug me close and say that to whom much is given, much is also expected. I needed him to smile at me, in that way that lit up his face, that warmed something inside me."[20]

Kambili's Road of Trials begins with her grandfather, who she sees but is not allowed to associate with because he's a pagan. She's invited along with her brother Jaja to stay at her Aunt Ifeoma's small apartment in Nsukka which "is uncivilized compared to Enugu," where her aunt lives with her two children, Obiora and Amaka.[21] Kambili sleeps with Amaka, who begrudgingly hosts her. Thus, Kambili travels a long distance far from her affluent world into an uncivilized territory where she faces self-hate, fear, and indecision. "I had felt as if I were not there, that I was just observing a table where you could say anything at any time to anyone, where the air was free for you to breathe as you wished."[22] She also begins a relationship with Father Amadi, the new priest.

As a quiet, shy girl, Kambili finally asserts herself when she's being bullied by her cousin, receiving an illusory Boon of success when her aunt notices appreciatively. "So your voice can be this loud."[23] Kambili is then Betrayed by her father who burns her feet as punishment for spending time with her heathen grandfather. She Descends when her father shreds the painting of her grandfather he finds with her, and Kambili falls to the floor to cradle the picture's remains in a fetal position. "I sank to the floor, lay on the pieces of paper."[24] Her father violently, physically abuses her as a consequence, and she spends Descent Dwelling in the hospital, in and out of consciousness, so close to death's door that she's given extreme unction. When she realizes that she's been in a hospital for a long time, she demands to see her Aunt Ifeoma, in a Yearning to Reconnect. Her father hires a female tutor who helps her prepare for her finals, in which she takes first place. Her classmates also stop by, having heard of her accident. "My class girls visited me that afternoon, their eyes wide with awed admiration."[25] Finally, she's taken to her aunt's house to complete her recuperation.

Kambili Heals the Mother/Child divide when her mother suddenly appears at her aunt's house, broken in body and spirit from her father's most recent attack. Kambili's mother miscarried again, and this time Kambili is able to console and mourn with her mother. "Mama slid down to the floor. She sat with her legs stretched out in front of her. It was so undignified, but I lowered myself and sat next to her, our shoulders touching. She cried for a long time. She cried until my hand, clasped in hers, felt stiff."[26] In Finding the Man with a Heart, Kambili's wounded masculine is healed in the death of her father, a taming of the family tyrant. When it's discovered that her mother had been poisoning him, her brother, a young boy who's grown into a man with a heart, steps forward, takes the blame and the punishment. Kambili experiences Union in carrying the words of Father Amadi close to her heart. "His letters dwell on me. I carry them around because they are long and detailed, because they remind me of my worthiness, because they tug at my feelings [. . .]. And I carry them with me, also, because they give me grace. [. . .] I no longer wonder if I have a right to love Father Amadi; I simply go ahead and love him."[27] Kambili also has a family reunion in visiting Jaja in prison along with her mother to deliver the news that he will soon be free. She reveals her state of Bliss in discussing new projects they will undertake, return to Nsukka, visit Aunt Ifeoma in America, and plant purple hibiscus. In the final scene, she is shown as a master of heaven and earth as she describes how she can touch the clouds. "[C]louds like dyed cotton wool hang low, so low I feel I can reach out and squeeze the moisture from them."[28] Thus, the heroine's journey is not another Western cultural import being used to conquer and subsume all others into the totalizing force of the same. It's an indigenous part of humanity that can be used in face-to-face encounters to trigger epiphanies of analectic moment.

In mythology, the monomyth rebooted is exemplified by the myth of Eros and Psyche, the novel *Jane Eyre*, and the film *Titanic*, where Eros, young Jane, and Jack embark on hero's journeys and Psyche, adult Jane, and Rose embark on heroine's journeys. This pattern can also be found and applied elsewhere, including biographies, memoirs, music, music videos, video games, paintings, comic books, audiobooks, sacred books, documentaries, television, podcasts, articles, and even speechwriting. And it's also in *Star Wars—Episode IV, A New Hope*.

   Luke Skywalker begins his journey in his Ordinary World of Tatooine, living a dull agrarian life in the hinterlands of a planet found on the outskirts of the Galactic Empire. The difference between the ordinary world he lives in and the extraordinary world he later enters is dramatic. At this step, in psychological terms, the hero becomes aware of the Self as perhaps something different than the Ego. While going about his chores, Skywalker inadvertently intercepts a message from Artoo for Obi-Wan Kenobi and wants to learn more about the woman asking for help, his Call to Adventure. He must seek out the recluse, Obi-Wan, a Jedi who knew Luke's father and still had his lightsaber. When Obi-Wan Kenobi invites Luke to join the quest to defeat the Galactic Empire, Luke Refuses the Call because he's responsible for the care of his uncle's crops. But when Luke returns home to find that his adoptive parents have been murdered and the crops burned, it becomes clear that he has no choice but to join the fight against the Empire.

   Having lost everything, Luke joins Obi-Wan, who becomes his Mentor, teaching him the ways of a Jedi. Together they cross a no-man's land to reach Mos Eisley in search of safe passage on a spaceship, which is a "wretched hive of scum and villain"[29] who serve as the nuisance threshold guardians, in Crossing the First Threshold. Meeting with Han Solo and Chewbacca, they gain Allies, while escaping stormtroopers on their way to meet Princess Leia. Luke begins his training to become a Jedi as they Approach the Inmost Cave through the Death Star, entering a mini-special world. He leaps into the Ordeal when they all jump down the garbage chute and face death by trash compaction. They are Rewarded for surviving death by escaping with the Death Star plans and the princess. On the Road Back, Leia rallies the dispirited troops, pulling family together after a death as Luke mourns Obi-Wan while escaping by magical flight. Han Solo sounds the alarm of a reversal of fortune when they are pursed by stormtroopers, the renewed threat by the story villain.

   At the rebel base, Luke joins the space fighters to attack the Death Star in a final showdown where he faces a difficult choice of using the navigation equipment or trusting his instincts. With Darth Vader homing in a kill shot, Luke comes close to death but is Resurrected by a surprise rescue from Han Solo. Against all logic, Luke shuts off his computer guide and uses the Force within him to successfully destroy the Death Star, proving to the audience that he has changed. By tapping into the Elixir of the Jedi Force, Luke shares it to win the battle against the Galactic Empire and be rewarded for his services.

   The heroic journey of Luke Skywalker has been so ingrained into our culture that it can be retold in five hundred words like a fairy tale and still resonate. But perhaps there was more to this story. As an androcentric society, we have been blinded by his pursuits as a masculine hero, but what if we shifted the paradigm and examined his journey symbolically from the perspective of a heroine's journey? In the beginning, there's a Separation from the Maternal, as reflected by Luke's separation from his mother, Queen Amidala, his home, homeland, and even his womb-mate. Luke grows up Over-Identifying with the Paternal through his uncle as a farmer to the extent that when he's called to action Luke refuses because he has farm chores. In addition, he identifies with his father, Anakin, when his aunt says, "he has too much of his father in him."[30] Forced out of his life, Luke embarks on a Road of Trials after his aunt and uncle are murdered. Han Solo represents an ogre who doesn't believe in Luke's quest, the rebellion, or the Jedi Force as they travel to Alderaan.

Luke experiences a Boon when he first uses "the Force" during his Jedi training. However, their expectations of meeting with Princess Leia are Betrayed when they discover that the planet of Alderaan was destroyed. A tractor beam from the Death Star forces them to Descend into its hollows. They hide in the bottom of the ship and later change into stormtrooper uniforms. Inside, Luke and Han Solo contrive to act as stormtroopers in the hopes of stealing the Death Star schematics. They Descent Dwell in the trash compactor where they face death, except for the opportune help of Luke's *sukkal*, left behind to save them if they ran into trouble. Rescued from the deep, Luke Yearns to Reconnect with Obi Wan as he watches Darth Vader kill his mentor. Luke takes time to heal and mourn. When he arrives at the rebel base, he Heals the Mother/Child Divide in the community of rebel fighters, even finding an old friend from Tatooine who has joined in the fight. He also embraces Leia, a maternal figure by virtue of being the daughter of his mother and a mother of the Rebel cause. In battling the tyrant, Darth Vader, Luke Finds the Man with a Heart by listening to the inspired voice of Kenobi to follow his heart to defeat Vader. In addition, Luke is rescued by a man with a heart, Han Solo. Luke achieves Union when he's reunited with Leia and Han Solo, savoring their victory. At the end, Luke experiences Bliss as he's anointed with the Medal of Bravery in the Great Temple of Yavin 4 before everyone for saving the Alliance.

Patriarchal Hollywood has only read the hero's journey into *Star Wars*, upholding it as the prime example of the mythic quest, the blockbuster to pattern all blockbusters. But perhaps George Lucas's true genius was not in writing the quintessential hero's journey but in writing *both*. He consciously conveys the hero's journey from the center while subconsciously delivering the heroine's journey from the periphery to showcase a deep, multi-layered, pluriversal, mythopoeic story. Where mythopoesis universalizes a lived experience, monomythic mythopoesis immortalizes it. Hence the enduring appeal of Eros and Psyche, *Jane Eyre*, and *Titanic*—years and, in the case of the former two, cultures and geographies away from its origins. The monomyth rebooted enables mythopoesis to portray the syzygy between the conscious and the unconscious, the Ego's return to the Self, the union of the internal hero and heroine of the psyche, the coming of age followed by the coming of middle age, and the intermentational, analectical epiphany required by the paradigm shift of transmodernity.

NOTES

1. Doty, "Joseph Campbell's Myth and/versus Religion," 436.

2. Jacobi, *The Way of Individuation*, 62.

3. Anthony Russo and Joe Russo, dir., *Avengers: Endgame* (Marvel Studios, 2019).

4. Joss Whedon, dir., *The Avengers* (Marvel Studios, 2012).

5. Nietzsche, *The Will to Power*, 541.

6. Queen, "Bohemian Rhapsody," in *A Night at the Opera* (EMI).

7. Queen, "Bohemian Rhapsody."; Simon & Garfunkel, "The Boxer," in *Bridge Over Troubled Water* (Columbia records, 1970).

8. Queen, "Bohemian Rhapsody."

9. Queen, "Bohemian Rhapsody."

10. Queen, "Bohemian Rhapsody."

11. Queen, "Bohemian Rhapsody."

12. Queen, "Bohemian Rhapsody."

13. Queen, "Bohemian Rhapsody."

14. Queen, "Bohemian Rhapsody."

15. Queen, "Bohemian Rhapsody."

16. Queen, "Bohemian Rhapsody."

17. Campbell, *Hero*, 238.

18. Chimamanda Ngozi Adichie, *Purple Hibiscus* (Chapel Hill: Algonquin Books of Chapel Hill, 2003).

19. Adichie, *Purple Hibiscus*, 35.

20. Adichie, *Purple Hibiscus*, 39.

21. Adichie, *Purple Hibiscus*, 116.

22. Adichie, *Purple Hibiscus*, 120.

23. Adichie, *Purple Hibiscus*, 170.

24. Adichie, *Purple Hibiscus*, 210.

25. Adichie, *Purple Hibiscus*, 215.

26. Adichie, *Purple Hibiscus*, 248.

27. Adichie, *Purple Hibiscus*, 303.

28. Adichie, *Purple Hibiscus*, 308.

29. George Lucas, Lawrence Kasdan, and Leigh Bracket, *Star Wars: The Annotated Screenplays*, ed. Laurent Bouzereau (New York: Ballantine Books, 1997).

30. George Lucas, dir., *Star Wars* (20th Century Fox, 1977).

Bibliography

Abraham, Karl. *Dreams and Myths: A Study in Race Psychology.* Translated by William A. White. New York: The Journal of Nervous and Mental Disease Publishing Company, 1913.

Adichie, Chimamanda Ngozi. *Purple Hibiscus.* Chapel Hill: Algonquin Books of Chapel Hill, 2003.

Adler, Alfred. *The Practice and Theory of Individual Psychology.* Translated by Paul Radin. 2nd ed. New York, London: Harcourt, K. Paul, Trench, Trubner & Co. Ltd., 1955.

Aliaga Lavrijsen, Jessica, and José María Yebra-Pertusa, eds. *Transmodern Perspectives on Contemporary Literatures in English,* vol. 29. New York: Routledge, 2019.

Apuleius. *Cupid & Psyche.* Edited by E. J. Kenney. Cambridge, New York: Cambridge University Press, 1990.

Apuleius, and Sarah Ruden. *The Golden Ass.* New Haven Conn.: Yale University Press, 2011.

Apuleius, Lucius. *Cupid & Psyche.* Edited by E. J. Kenney. Cambridge & New York: Cambridge University Press, 1990.

———. *The Metamorphoses, or Golden Ass of Apuleius of Madaura.* Translated by Harold Edgeworth Butler. 2 vols. Oxford: Clarendon Press, 1910.

Barthes, Roland, and Stephen Heath. *Image, Music, Text.* New York: Hill and Wang, 1977.

Baulsom, Brian T. M.N.F.S.H. *The Cycle of Growth.* Accessed September 6, 2020. www.cycleofgrowth.com.

Beaumont-Thomas, Ben. "Queen's Bohemian Rhapsody Becomes Most Streamed Song from the 20th Century." *The Guardian,* December 11, 2018. https://www.theguardian.com/music/2018/dec/11/queen-bohemian-rhapsody-most-streamed-song-20th-century.

Beauvoir, Simone de. *The Second Sex.* Translated by H. M. Parshley. New York: Alfred A. Knopf, 1993.

Beebe, Maurice. *Ivory Towers and Sacred Founts: The Artist as Hero in Fiction from Goethe to Joyce.* New York: New York University Press, 1964.

Benhabib, Seyla. *Situating the Self: Gender, Community, and Postmodernism in Contemporary Ethics.* New York: Routledge, 1992.

Block, Alex Ben. "George Lucas Will Use Disney \$4 Billion to Fund Education." *The Hollywood Reporter*, October 12, 2012. https://www.hollywoodreporter.com/news/general-news/disney-deal-george-lucas-will-384947/.

Bolen, Jean Shinoda. *Goddesses in Everywoman: Powerful Archetypes in Women's Lives.* 1st Quill ed. New York: Quill, 2004.

Bond, Sarah E., and Joel Christensen. "The Man Behind the Myth: Should We Question the Hero's Journey." *LA Review of Books* (https://lareviewofbooks.org/article/the-man-behind-the-myth-should-we-question-the-heros-journey/), August 12, 2021.

Brontë, Charlotte. *Jane Eyre.* repr. New York, London: Harper, 1899. London: Smith, Elder, 1847.

Burns, Kevin. *Empire of Dreams: The Story of the Star Wars Trilogy.* 20th Century Fox Television, 2004.

———. *Star Wars: The Legacy Revealed.* Prometheus Entertainment, The History Channel, and Lucasfilm Ltd, 2007. Documentary.

Bursi, Adam Collins. "Holy Spit and Magic Spells: Religion, Magic, and the Body in Late Ancient Judaism, Christianity, and Islam." PhD diss., Cornell University, 2015.

Butler, Judith. *Gender Trouble: Feminism and the Subversion of Identity.* New York: Routledge, 1990.

———. "Sex and Gender in Simone de Beauvoir's 'Second Sex.'" *Yale French Studies* 72 (1987): 35.

Cameron, James, dir. 1997. *Titanic.* United States: Paramount Pictures.

Cameron, James. *Titanic: James Cameron's Illustrated Screenplay.* New York: HarperPerennial, 1998.

Campbell, Joseph. *The Hero with a Thousand Faces.* Novato: New World Library, 2008.

———. *The Hero with a Thousand Faces.* 2nd ed. Princeton: Princeton University Press, 1968.

———. *The Inner Reaches of Outer Space: Metaphor as Myth and as Religion.* Novato: New World Library, 2002.

———. *The Masks of God: Creative Mythology.* 4 vols. New York: Arkana, 1991.

Campbell, Joseph, and Bill D. Moyers. *The Power of Myth.* New York: Doubleday, 1988.

Carpenter, Humphrey. *J. R. R. Tolkien: A Biography.* London: G. Allen & Unwin, 1978.

Claremont de Castillejo, Irene. *Knowing Woman: A Feminine Psychology.* New York: Putnam, 1973.

Clark, Isabelle. "The Gamos of Hera." In *The Sacred and The Feminine in Ancient Greece*, edited by Sue Blundell and Margaret Williamson. London & New York: Routledge, 1998.

Collins, Robert G. "*Star Wars*: The Pastiche of Myth and the Yearning for a Past Future." *Journal of Popular Culture* 11, no. 1 (Summer 1977): 1.

De Tocqueville, Alexis. *Democracy in America.* Translated by Henry Reeve. Edited by Francis Bowen. London: Wordsworth, 1998.

Descartes, R., and N.K. Smith. *Descartes Philosophical Writings.* New York: Modern Library, 1958.

Doty, William G. "Joseph Campbell's Myth and/Versus Religion." *Soundings: An Interdisciplinary Journal* 79, no. 3-4 (1996): 421–45.

————. *Mythography: The Study of Myths and Rituals.* 2nd ed. Tuscaloosa: University of Alabama Press, 2000.

Dover, K. J. *Greek Homosexuality.* London: Duckworth, 1978.

Durkheim, Emile. *The Elementary Forms of Religious Life.* Translated by Karen E. Fields. New York: Free Press, 1995.

Dussel, Enrique. "A New Age in the History of Philosophy: The World Dialogue between Philosophical Traditions." *Philosophy & Social Criticism* 35, no. 5 (2009): 499–516. https://doi.org/10.1177/0191453709103424.

————. *Ethics of Liberation in the Age of Globalization and Exclusion.* Translated by Alejandro A. Vallega. Durham: Duke University Press, 2013.

————. *Philosophy of Liberation.* Maryknoll: Orbis Books, 1985.

————. "World-System and 'Trans'-Modernity." *Nepantla* 3, no. 2 (2002): 221–44.

Edinger, Edward. *The Aion Lectures: Exploring the Self in C.G. Jung's Aion.* Toronto: Inner City Books, 1996.

————. *Ego and Archetype: Individuation and the Religious Runction of the Psyche.* Edited by C. G. Jung Foundation for Analytical Psychology. New York: Putnam, 1972.

Eliade, Mircea. *Cosmos and History: The Myth of the Eternal Return.* New York: Harper, 1959.

————. *Myth and Reality.* New York: Harper & Row, 1963.

Elliott, J. K., and M. R. James. *The Apocryphal New Testament: A Collection of Apocryphal Christian Literature in an English Translation.* Oxford: Oxford University Press, 1993. doi:10.1093/0198261829.001.0001.

Eppard, Lawrence M., Mark R. Rank, Heather E. Bullock, Noam Chomsky, Henry A. Giroux, David Brady, and Dan Schubert. *Rugged Individualism and the Misunderstanding of American Inequality.* Bethlehem: Lehigh University Press, 2020.

Estés, Clarissa Pinkola. *Women Who Run with the Wolves: Myths and Stories of the Wild Woman Archetype.* New York: Ballantine Books, 1992.

Fanon, Frantz. *Black Skin, White Masks.* New York: Grove Press, 1967.

Felser, Joseph M. "Was Joseph Campbell a Postmodernist." *Journal of the American Academy of Religion* 64, no. 2 (1996): 395–417.

Fimi, Dimitra. "Later Fantasy Fiction: Tolkien's Legacy." In *A Companion to J. R. R. Tolkien,* edited by Stuart D. Lee. Malden: Wiley Blackwell, 2014.

Foucault, Michel. *Discipline and Punish: The Birth of the Prison.* Translated by Alan Sheridan. 2nd ed. New York: Vintage Books, 1995.

Franz, Marie-Louise von. *The Feminine in Fairy Tales.* Rev. ed. Boston, New York: Shambhala, 1993.

————. *The Golden Ass of Apuleius: The Liberation of the Feminine in Man.* rev. ed. Boston: Shambhala Publications, 1992.

Freud, Sigmund. *Totem and Taboo: Resemblances between the Psychic Lives of Savages and Neurotics.* Translated by A. A. Brill. New York: Moffat, Yard and Company, 1918.

Girardot, N.J. "Initiation and Meaning in the Tale of Snow White and the Seven Dwarfs." *The Journal of American Folklore* 90, No. 357 (1977): 274–300.

Grosfoguel, Ramón. "World-Systems Analysis in the Context of Transmodernity, Border Thinking, and Global Coloniality." *Review - Fernand Braudel Center for the Study of Economies, Historical Systems, and Civilizations* 29, no. 2 (2006): 167–87.

Hamilton, Edith. *Mythology.* repr. Boston: Back Bay Books, 1998. Boston: Little, Brown, 1942.

Hanks, Patrick, Kate Hardcastle, and Flavia Hodges. *A Dictionary of First Names.* Oxford Reference. Edited by Kate Hardcastle and Flavia Hodges. 2nd ed. Oxford & New York: Oxford University Press, 2006.

Hannah, Barbara. *Encounters with the Soul: Active Imagination as Developed by C.G. Jung.* Wilmette: Chiron Publications, 2001.

Hegel, Georg Wilhelm Friedrich, and Johannes Hoffmeister. *Lectures on the Philosophy of World History: Introduction, Reason in History.* Cambridge, New York: Cambridge University Press, 1975.

Hill, Gareth. *Masculine and Feminine: The Natural Flow of Opposites in the Psyche.* 1st ed. Boston: Shambhala, 1992.

Hillman, James. *Healing Fiction.* Dallas: Spring Publications, 1994.

———. *The Myth of Analysis: Three Essays in Archetypal Psychology.* Evanston: Northwestern University Press, 1972.

———. *Re-Visioning Psychology.* New York: Harper Colophon Books, 1977.

———. *The Soul's Code: In Search of Character and Calling.* New York: Ballantine Books, 2017.

Hirsch, Marianne. "The Novel of Formation as Genre: Between *Great Expectations* and *Lost Illusions* in Studies in the Novel." *Genre* 12, no. 3 (1979): 293–311.

Horkheimer, Max, and Theodor W. Adorno. *Dialectic of Enlightenment.* Translated by Edmund Jephcott. Stanford: Stanford University Press, 2002.

———. *Dialectic of Enlightenment.* New York: Herder and Herder, 1972.

Horner, James, and Céline Dion. "My Heart Will Go on (Love Theme from *Titanic*)." In *Titanic Music from the Motion Picture*. New York: Sony Classical, 1997. sound recording.

Jacobi, Jolande. "The Process of Individuation." *Journal of Analytical Psychology* 111, no. 2 (1958): 95–114. https://doi.org/10.1111/j.1465-5922.1958.00095.x.

———. *The Way of Individuation.* New York: Harcourt, 1967.

Johnson, Robert A. *She: Understanding Feminine Psychology.* rev. ed. New York: Perennial Library, 1989.

Jung, C. G. "Aion: Researches into the Phenomenology of the Self," *The Collected Works of C.G. Jung.* Edited by Herbert Read, Michael Fordham, Gerhard Adler and William McGuire. 2nd ed. Vol. 9, Part 2, Princeton: Princeton University Press, 1968.

———. "The Archetypes and the Collective Unconscious," *The Collected Works of C. G. Jung, Volume 9, Part 1*(1980): xi, 451 p., 78 p. of plates.

———. "Man and His Symbols." Edited by Marie-Luise von Franz. Garden City: Doubleday, 1964.

———. "Psychological Types." *The Collected Works of C. G. Jung,* Vol. 6. Rev. ed. Princeton: Princeton University Press, 1976.

———. "Psychology and Alchemy." *Collected Works*. 2nd ed. Princeton: Princeton University Press, 1968.

———. "Psychology and Class of Religion: West and East," In *The Collected Works of C. G. Jung*, vol. 11,(1969).

———. "The Structure and Dynamics of the Psyche," In *The Collected Works of C. G. Jung*, vol. 8,,(1969): x, 597 p.

———. "The Symbolic Life: Miscellaneous Writings," *Collected Works of C G Jung*. Princeton, N.J.: Princeton University Press, 1976.

———. "Symbols of Transformation: An Analysis of the Prelude to a Case of Schizophrenia," In *The Collected Works of C. G. Jung*, vol. 5,(1962).

———. "Two Essays on Analytical Psychology," In *The Collected Works of C. G. Jung,* vol. 7,(1966): xi, 349 p.

Jung, C. G., and Joan Chodorow. *Jung on Active Imagination.* Princeton: Princeton University Press, 1997.

Kant, Immanuel, Pauline Kleingeld, Jeremy Waldron, Michael W. Doyle, and Allen W. Wood. *Toward Perpetual Peace and Other Writings on Politics, Peace, and History.* New Haven: Yale University Press, 2006.

Kline, Morris. *Mathematics: The Loss of Certainty.* New York: Oxford University Press, 1980.

Kramer, Samuel Noah. *Sumerian Mythology: A Study of Spiritual and Literary Achievement in the Third Millennium B.C.* Rev. ed. New York: Harper, 1961.

———. *The Sumerians: Their History, Culture, and Character.* Chicago: University of Chicago Press, 1963.

Kristeva, Julia. *Strangers to Ourselves.* New York: Columbia University Press, 1991.

Kristeva, Julia, and Kelly Oliver. *The Portable Kristeva.* New York: Columbia University Press, 1997.

Labouvie-Vief, Gisela. *Psyche and Eros: Mind and Gender in the Life Course.* Cambridge & New York: Cambridge University Press, 1994.

Larrington, Carolyne. *The Feminist Companion to Mythology.* London: Pandora Press, 1992.

Lasch, Christopher. *The True and Only Heaven: Progress and Its Critics.* New York: W.W. Norton & Company, 1991.

Lerner, Gerda. *The Creation of Patriarchy.* New York: Oxford University Press, 1986.

Lévi-Strauss, Claude. *Myth and Meaning.* Toronto, Buffalo: University of Toronto Press, 1978.

———. *The Naked Man.* New York: Harper & Row, 1981.

Lévinas, Emmanuel. *Collected Philosophical Papers.* Translated by Alphonso Lingis. Phaenomenologica. Dordrecht: Martinus Nijhoff Publishers, 1987.

———. *Ethics and Infinity.* Translated by Richard A. Cohen. Pittsburgh: Duquesne University Press, 1985.

———. *Totality and Infinity: An Essay on Exteriority.* Pittsburgh: Duquesne University Press, 1969.

Lowenthal, Martin. *Alchemy of the Soul: The Eros and Psyche Myth as a Guide to Transformation.* Berwick: Nicolas-Hays, 2004.

Lucas, George, dir. 1977. *Star Wars: Episode IV - A New Hope*. United States: 20th Century Fox.

Lucas, George, Lawrence Kasdan, and Leigh Bracket. *Star Wars: The Annotated Screenplays*. Edited by Laurent Bouzereau. New York: Ballantine Books, 1997.

Lyden, John C. "Whose Film Is It, Anyway? Canonicity and Authority in *Star Wars* Fandom." *Journal of the American Academy of Religion* 80, no. 3 (2012): 775–86. https://doi.org/10.1093/jaarel/lfs037.

Lyotard, Jean-François. *The Postmodern Condition: A Report on Knowledge*. Minneapolis: University of Minnesota Press, 1984.

Magazine, LA Times. "The Southern California Woman, on the Job, Making It, the Personal Stories of Six Women Who Have Found Success in Individual Ways: Jill Barad, Corporation Executive." *Los Angeles Times* 4 December 1988. Accessed 6 September 2017. http://articles.latimes.com/1988-12-04/magazine/tm-1687_1 _jill-barad.

Malinowski, Bronislaw, and Robert Redfield. *Magic, Science and Religion, and Other Essays*. Boston: Beacon Press, 1948.

McNary, Dave. "*Star Wars* Movies Push Overall Licensed Merchandise Sales to $262 Billion." *Variety*. (May 22, 2017). Accessed March 2, 2023. https://variety .com/2017/film/news/star-wars-movies-licensed-merchandise-1202438161/.

Merleau-Ponty, Maurice. *Phenomenology of Perception*. London, New York: Routledge, 1962.

Mignolo, Walter D. "The Geopolitics of Knowledge and the Colonial Difference." *The South Atlantic Quarterly* 101, no. 1 (2002): 57–96. https://doi.org/10.1215 /00382876-101-1-57.

Mills, Frederick B. *Enrique Dussel's Ethics of Liberation: An Introduction*. Cham: Palgrave Macmillan, 2018. doi:10.1007/978-3-319-94550-7.

"Mstislav Keldysh Family History." accessed September 6, 2017, <http://www .famhist.ru/famhist/schelkin/0006952a.htm>.

Murdock, Maureen. *The Heroine's Journey: Woman's Quest for Wholeness*. Boston, New York: Shambhala, 1990.

Nagel, Ernest, and James Roy Newman. *Gödel's Proof*. New York: New York University Press, 1958.

Nasr, Seyyed Hossein. *The Study Quran: A New Translation and Commentary*. New York: HarperOne, 2015.

Neumann, Erich. *Amor and Psyche: The Psychic Development of the Feminine, a Commentary on the Tale by Apuleius*. Translated by Ralph Manheim. repr. Princeton: Princeton University Press, 1971. New York: Pantheon, 1956.

Nietzsche, Friedrich Wilhelm. *The Birth of Tragedy; or Hellenism and Pessimism*. 3rd ed. London: George Allen and Unwin Ltd, 1923.

———. *The Will to Power*. Translated by R. J. Wilhelm Kaufmann and Walter Arnold Hollingdale. New York: Vintage Books, 1968.

Ogden, Daniel. *Magic, Witchcraft, and Ghosts in the Greek and Roman Worlds: A Sourcebook*. Oxford; New York: Oxford University Press, 2002.

Pearson, Carol. *Persephone Rising: Awakening the Heroine Within*. New York: HarperElixir, 2015.

Pearson, Carol, and Katherine Pope. *The Female Hero in American and British Literature.* New York: Bowker, 1981.

Perera, Sylvia Brinton. *Descent to the Goddess: A Way of Initiation for Women.* Toronto: Inner City Books, 1981.

Pratt, Annis. *Archetypal Patterns in Women's Fiction.* Bloomington: Indiana University Press, 1981.

Qualls-Corbett, Nancy. *Awakening Woman: Dreams and Individuation.* Toronto: Inner City Books, 2002.

Queen. "Bohemian Rhapsody." *A Night at the Opera (*EMI, 1975).

"Queen's 'Bohemian Rhapsody' Becomes Oldest Music Video to Get a Billion Youtube Views." *Variety.* https://variety.com/2019/music/news/queen-bohemian -rhapsody-video-youtube-billion-record-1203275069/.

Rank, Otto. *The Myth of the Birth of the Hero: A Psychological Interpretation of Mythology.* Translated by F. Robbins and Smith Ely Jelliffe. New York: The Journal of Nervous and Mental Disease Publishing Company, 1914.

Rinzler, J. W. *The Making of Star Wars (Enhanced Edition).* New York: Random House Worlds, 2013.

———. *The Making of Star Wars, the Empire Strikes Back: The Definitive Story.* New York: Del Rey Books, 2010.

Ruan, Fangfu, and Molleen Matsumura. *Sex in China: Studies in Sexology in Chinese Culture.* Perspectives in Sexuality. New York: Plenum Press, 1991.

Russell, Bertrand. *History of Western Philosophy and Its Connection with Political and Social Circumstances from the Earliest Times to the Present Day.* London: G. Allen and Unwin ltd, 1946.

Russo, Anthony Russo and Joe. *Avengers: Endgame.* Marvel Studios, 2019.

Said, Edward W. *Culture and Imperialism.* New York: Vintage Books, 1994.

———. *Orientalism.* New York: Vintage Books, 1979.

Sardar, Ziauddin. *Postmodernism and the Other: The New Imperialism of Western Culture.* London, Sterling: Pluto Press, 1998.

Segal, Robert Alan. *Joseph Campbell: An Introduction.* repr. New York: Mentor Books, 1990. New York: Garland Pub., 1987.

Silva, Francisco Vaz da. "The Invention of Fairy Tales." *The Journal of American folklore* 123, no. 490 (2010): 398–425. https://doi.org/10.1353/jaf.2010.0001.

Simon and Garfunkel. "The Boxer." In *Bridge Over Troubled Water*, Columbia records, 1970.

Singer, June. *Androgyny: Toward a New Theory of Sexuality.* Garden City: Anchor Press, 1976.

Stein, Murray, and Lionel Corbett, eds. *Psyche's Stories: Modern Jungian Interpretations of Fairy Tales.* 3 vols. Vol. 1. Wilmette: Chiron Publications, 1995.

Tatar, Maria. *The Heroine with 1001 Faces.* New York: Liveright Publishing Corporation, 2021.

Temple, Robert K. G. *He Who Saw Everything: A Verse Translation of the Epic of Gilgamesh.* London: Rider, 1991.

Thompson, Simon. "Queen's 'Bohemian Rhapsody' Is Officially the World's Most-Streamed Song." *Forbes*, December 10, 2018. https://www.forbes.com/sites

/simonthompson/2018/12/10/queens-bohemian-rhapsody-is-officially-the-worlds
-most-streamed-song/?sh=6b14c1bcc1f0.

Tolkien, J. R. R. *Tree and Leaf: Including Mythopoeia and the Homecoming of Beorhtnoth.* London: Harper Collins Publishers, 1988.

"Top Lifetime Adjusted Grosses." Box Office Mojo by IMDB Pro, Updated March 2, 2023, accessed March 2, 2023, https://www.boxofficemojo.com/chart/top_lifetime _gross_adjusted/?adjust_gross_to=2022.

"Top Lifetime Grosses (Worldwide)." Box Office Mojo by IMDB Pro, Updated March 5, 2023, accessed March 5, 2023, https://www.boxofficemojo.com/chart/ top_lifetime_gross/?area=XWW.

Turner, Victor W. *The Ritual Process: Structure and Anti-Structure.* Chicago: Aldine Pub. Co., 1969.

Ulanov, Ann Belford. *The Feminine in Jungian Psychology and in Christian Theology.* Evanston: Northwestern University Press, 1971.

Varsamopoulou, Evy. *The Poetics of the Kunstlerinroman and the Aesthetics of the Sublime.* Aldershot; Burlington: Ashgate, 2002.

Vogler, Christopher. *The Writer's Journey: Mythic Structure for Writers.* 3rd ed. Studio City: Michael Wiese Productions, 2007.

Whedon, Joss. *The Avengers.* Marvel Studios, 2012.

Whitmont, Edward C. *Return of the Goddess.* New York: Crossroad, 1982.

———. *The Symbolic Quest: Basic Concepts of Analytical Psychology.* 2nd ed. Princeton: Princeton University Press, 1991.

Wolkstein, Diane, and Samuel Noah Kramer. *Inanna, Queen of Heaven and Earth: Her Stories and Hymns from Sumer.* New York: Harper & Row, 1983.

Woodman, Marion, and Elinor Dickson. *Dancing in the Flames: The Dark Goddess in the Transformation of Consciousness.* Boston: Shambhala, 1996.

Xiang, Zairong. *Queer Ancient Ways: A Decolonial Exploration.* Santa Barbara: Punctum Books, 2018.

Zaleski, Philip, and Carol Zaleski. *The Fellowship: The Literary Lives of the Inklings: J.R.R. Tolkien, C. S. Lewis, Owen Barfield, Charles Williams.* New York: Farrar, Straus and Giroux, 2015.

Index

About the Author

As a mythopoeic scholar, **Nadia Salem** researches mythic structures in narrative throughout literature and film. By understanding mythology's influence in creating classics, bestsellers, and blockbusters, she studies cross-cultural, genre-bending, marginalized stories for popular and political impact. Nadia Salem has a doctorate in English and Creative Writing from Aberystwyth University and a doctorate in law from Northwestern University Pritzker School of Law. Her academic interests are in law and literature, mythopoesis, and transmodernism. She has taught mythic structure at Georgetown University and Northwestern University and currently serves as faculty at DePaul University. Nadia Salem is also a produced playwright, having authored several plays about the American immigrant BIPOC experience.

www.ingramcontent.com/pod-product-compliance
Lightning Source LLC
Chambersburg PA
CBHW062038270326
41929CB00014B/2467